Textual Analysis for English Language & Literature

Skills for Success

Carolyn P. Henly
Angela Stancar Johnson

HODDER
EDUCATION
AN HACHETTE UK COMP

Carrie: With many thanks to my husband for his unending patience with my many projects.

Angela: I would like to dedicate this book to Adrian, Ella, Freya and Oskar – my in-house support team.

Orders: please contact Bookpoint Ltd, 130 Park Drive, Milton Park, Abingdon, Oxon OX14 4SE. Telephone: +44 (0)1235 827827. Fax: +44 (0)1235 400401. Email education@bookpoint.co.uk Lines are open from 9 a.m. to 5 p.m., Monday to Saturday, with a 24-hour message answering service. You can also order through our website: www.hoddereducation.com

ISBN: 9781510467156

© Carolyn P. Henly and Angela Stancar Johnson 2019

First published in 2019 by
Hodder Education,
An Hachette UK Company
Carmelite House
50 Victoria Embankment
London EC4Y 0DZ

www.hoddereducation.com

Impression number   10 9 8 7 6 5 4 3 2

Year   2023 2022 2021 2020

Cover photo © sveta - stock.adobe.com

Typeset by Integra Software Services Pvt. Ltd., Pondicherry, India

Printed in Spain

A catalogue record for this title is available from the British Library.

Contents

How to use this book

This book is focused on helping you build and develop your skills in textual analysis. The main literary genres will be covered, as well as many of the most common non-literary text types. You will have the opportunity to examine texts or extracts which focus on certain literary aspects and conventions of these text types. Some of the non-literary texts that are included have appeared on past exam papers, so the book also serves as an anthology of the types of texts that you may encounter in your final examination.

The main focus of this book is on developing your skills in unseen textual analysis, which is the basis of Paper 1; however, many of the activities are also applicable to the texts that you will be studying within the classroom. Therefore, the skills targeted here can be applied in a variety of contexts. The book is designed to be used independently by students or in a more guided teacher-led approach.

Features of this book

There are some features you should look for throughout the book to help with your understanding of textual analysis.

KEY TERMS

These are highlighted to give you access to vocabulary you need for each topic. These terms are also included in the glossary.

TECHNIQUES, FEATURES AND TIPS

These boxes provide handy tips and guidance on how to identify features of a text.

ACTIVITY

Activities are designed to test your understanding of each topic and provide practice to develop your skills for the exam.

■ Using QR codes

Look out for the QR codes throughout the book. They are placed in the margin alongside weblinks for quick scanning (as shown in the list opposite).

To use the QR codes to access the web links you will need a QR code reader for your smartphone/tablet. There are many free readers available, depending on the device that you use. We have supplied some suggestions below, but this is not an exhaustive list and you should only download software compatible with your device and operating system. We do not endorse any of the third-party products listed and downloading them is at your own risk.

- For iPhone/iPad, Qrafter – **https://itunes.apple.com/us/app/qrafter-qr-code/id416098700?mt=8**

- For Android, QR Droid – **https://play.google.com/store/apps/details?id=la.droid.qr&hl=en**

- For Blackberry, QR Code Scanner – **https://appworld.blackberry.com/webstore/content/19908464/?lang=en**

- For Windows/Symbian, Upcode – **www.microsoft.com/en-gb/p/upcode/9nblggh081ps?rtc=1&activetab=pivot:overviewtab**

Notes on the activities

Remember that textual analysis is not a science. Interpretation is largely about developing a personal response to the text rather than arriving at a definitive answer, and therefore each interpretation may be slightly different. As long as your interpretation is supported by the language of the text, that is okay. The notes on the activities, which appear at the back of the book should not be viewed as conclusive; they are merely included to provide you with some possibilities of analysis and interpretation.

About the authors

Carolyn P. Henly (A.B. M.Ed, National Board Certification 2001, 2011) has recently retired after 33 years of teaching, 20 of those in the International Baccalaureate Programme. She has taught English HL, Theory of Knowledge, and IB Philosophy. She has served in a number of roles in the IB, including coordinator, examiner (both TOK and English), workshop leader, President of the Mid-Atlantic subregional organization, and member of two TOK curriculum review committees. She co-authored the third edition of the *Theory of Knowledge* textbook (Hodder Education), and series edited both *Language and Literature for the IB Diploma* and *English Literature for the IB Diploma* (Hodder Education) as well as contributing as author in the latter.

Angela Stancar Johnson (B.A., M.A., M.Ed.) is Head of English at Southbank International School in London, where she has taught all grades and levels of MYP English Language & Literature, DP English A, and Theory of Knowledge since 2009. Prior to that, she taught English and journalism in US public schools. Angela has served as an examiner for DP English and currently examines the MYP Interdisciplinary eAssessment and Personal Project. She co-authored the *Personal Project for the IB MYP 4 & 5: Skills for Success* and *Community Project for the IB MYP 3 & 4: Skills for Success* textbooks and contributed to *English Literature for the IB Diploma*, all published by Hodder Education.

Carolyn and Angela also authored *Literary Analysis for English Literature for the IB Diploma: Skills for Success* (Hodder Education, 2019).

1 What is textual analysis?

What is a text?

When you think of a text, you might think of something written. However, in the context of the Language A: Language and Literature course, a *text* is defined as anything from which information can be extracted, and includes the widest range of oral, written and visual materials present in society. This range will include single and multiple images with or without text, literary and non-literary written texts and extracts, media texts (for example, films), radio and television programmes and their scripts, and electronic texts that share aspects of a number of these areas (for example, video-sharing websites, web pages, SMS messages, blogs, wikis and tweets). Oral texts will include readings, speeches, broadcasts and transcriptions of recorded conversation.

What is textual analysis?

Analyse is one of the 18 IB Diploma Programme command terms, and it means to 'break down in order to bring out the essential elements or structure. To identify parts and relationships, and to interpret information to reach conclusions.' Textual analysis is the systematic examination of a text or aspect(s) of a text – a consideration of how the individual parts contribute to the whole. Textual analysis is not just about identifying *what* stylistic devices a writer uses; it is about exploring the effects of those devices. For example, does the use of a rhetorical device target a specific **audience** or suggest a specific **purpose**? Does the choice of a particular word evoke a certain **mood** or reflect the writer's or speaker's attitude? Textual analysis is about moving beyond the surface level of a text and exploring different layers of meaning which are created through language.

Textual analysis is a skill that can be learned and developed. Students who are intimidated by the process often view a text as a puzzle that needs to be solved. Textual analysis is not about guessing what an author *might* have meant. Instead, it is about developing an appreciation for the thought and feeling expressed in a text, and this is achieved through an understanding and appreciation of the language of the text itself.

■ Analysing texts: Key considerations

You will encounter a wide variety of texts throughout your study of Language and Literature, each with their own unique characteristics. We will cover some of the most common texts and their key characteristics in the following chapters, but there are certain elements shared by all texts, literary or non-literary. You can consider these aspects 'lenses' through which to view texts.

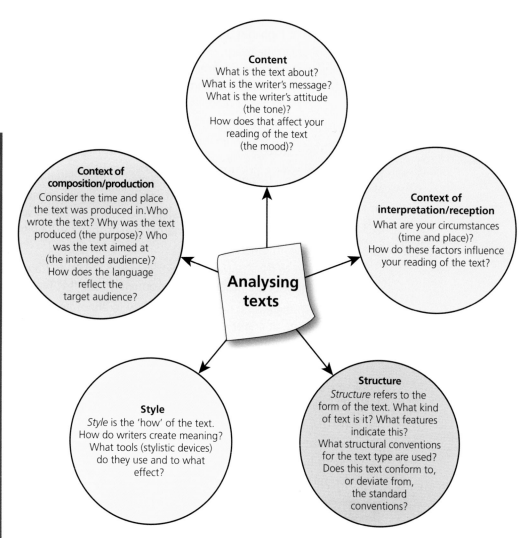

KEY TERMS

Semantic fields – a collection of words or phrases that are related to each other in meaning and connotation, for example, safety, welcome, support, shelter, structure and warmth would all be part of the same semantic field in relation to the word home.

Lexical sets – a group of words that are related to each other in meaning, for example, leaf, green, trunk, bark and branch would all be part of the same lexical set in relation to the word 'tree'.

Diction – the words chosen in a text.

Tone – the attitude of the writer or speaker towards his or her subject.

Figurative language – language that uses figures of speech, such as metaphors or symbols, to embellish meaning beyond the literal.

At all times, you should be asking yourself: how does the language of the text shape its meaning? This close examination of the text will allow you to move beyond a descriptive level to a more interpretive level.

Engaging with texts

In order to write convincingly about texts, you need to fully engage with them. This means actively reading, making notes, asking questions and developing a personal response to the text.

One of the best ways to engage with texts is to annotate as you read. Effective annotation is like having a dialogue with the text. You are noting down first impressions, posing questions and suggesting possible interpretations (which may or may not change as you read further – and as you read again).

ANNOTATION TIPS

✔ Do not try to underline or highlight everything. Focus on key words and phrases, especially those that seem to form a pattern. Look for **semantic fields** and **lexical sets**.

✔ Focus on style, especially **diction**. Colour code your markings according to word type. For example, you could highlight persuasive language in blue, words that reflect **tone** in pink, words associated with a particular theme in green and examples of **figurative language** in orange.

✔ Underline or highlight unfamiliar words or phrases. You will not have the benefit of a dictionary in the exam, but you can try to rely on context to help you work out meaning. Defining and learning the words in the texts you study in class will help you be better prepared for dealing with an unseen text; the bigger and more varied your vocabulary, the better reader you will be.

✔ Try to sum up a section of the text in one or two sentences in the margin. Summarizing in your own words can help you reach a deeper understanding of the text.

✔ Ask questions! If something confuses you, write it down in the margin of the text. Often the act of posing a question can help you work towards an understanding of the text; this is called *interrogating* the text. If you can't work out the answer for yourself, having noted it in the margin means that it will be there for you to raise in a discussion with others.

✔ You could use the Content/Context/Style and Structure framework to shape, or categorize, your annotations, if appropriate to the text type.

✔ Ultimately, there is no right or wrong way to annotate a text. Annotation is about engagement, and everyone engages differently. This engagement will guide you towards a personal connection with, and interpretation of, the text.

Look at the following text that a student has annotated. This is an opinion piece from the UK's *The Guardian* newspaper and is an example of the type of text you might encounter on Paper 1. Consider the student's thinking process or the strategies that they have used. What seems to be the focus? As you read the text yourself, you may pick up on things that the student has seemingly missed. The point of annotation is not to cover everything but to make initial observations which can lead to further insights.

ANNOTATION KEY

✔ Pink: Colloquial language (casual, friendly tone is in contrast to the serious point the author is making).

✔ Blue: Rhetorical questions.

✔ Green: Enumeration (persuasive technique).

✔ Yellow: Facts and figures (logos – see page 9 later in this chapter, and page 27 in Chapter 2).

There is use of idioms and metaphors throughout the text. These features of language add 'flavour' to a language, which is the case that the author is making for learning new languages, but they are also difficult for non-native speakers to understand. Motive?

To speak another language isn't just cultured, it's a blow against stupidity

Michael Hofmann

A leading translator argues that if we rely solely on English we'll lose the curiosity that drove Milton and Orwell

Sun 15 Aug 2010 00.06 BST

Schools and schoolchildren ditch languages like there's no tomorrow. Just as we've become adept at finding the shortest and the quickest and the most economical, so we can sniff out anything that's not a doss. 'Grammar? Pronunciation? Different alphabet? Spelling? Accents? Umlauts? Ooh, no thanks – don't fancy that.'

Quoted phrases and use of parentheses add to the colloquial tone.

The 'fascination of what's difficult' may be Yeats, but it's a long time since it's had much pull as an idea. Modern languages have become, in the awful semi-euphemism 'twilight subjects' – you study them on your own, after school's out.

Auf Wiedersehen, Dept, as the witticism goes. (German suffers especially badly. Numbers taking it have halved in seven years.) At 60% of state schools, three-quarters of 14-year-olds are not taking a modern language. Meanwhile, the take-up in primary schools is mysteriously delayed. Language teachers are not so easy to find and, indeed, where would they come from, given that no one's studying languages any more? Employers are becoming unhappy; their science and business and IT agenda has been overplayed.

It turns out that these 'redundant' languages can be jolly useful after all; only now it's much easier to find foreign nationals with English than Brits with another language. EU jobs earmarked for Britons are left unfilled because the entrance exams – another 'French plot' – are supposed to be taken in a second language; the new foreign secretary duly harrumphs across to Brussels to level the playing field (i.e. remove these irritating goalposts) with that mixture of put-upon and self-righteous that we get from our politicians when they ought to be feeling and expressing straightforward shame.

It looks like an education problem, but it's not an education problem. Education is just where things get shunted that society doesn't want to deal with or can't deal with. A dangerous dearth of respect in society? Let them teach it at school (don't ask me how, call it civics). That drearily prevalent, invertedly snobbish contempt for articulacy? More, better English lessons. An insufficiently integrated immigrant population? History. No sense of other people, other cultures, other languages? Go back to teaching the languages.

Education is a field hospital, where the little troops are patched up and turned round and sent back to fight in the great economic war that seems to be all that's left of life. Respect, articulateness and awareness of others are all related and what greater disrespect can there be than not speaking to others in their languages? Not even thinking of it? Not even being embarrassed about not thinking it?

Junking the requirement to learn, at 14, just past the age of crayons. How much respect does that bespeak? How much respect does that even allow? How can you hope to understand others while requiring them to speak to you in their English?

Appeal to logic (logos).

On the global political level, think of the blundering, insular, peremptory and oddly irrelevant posture of the Anglo-American powers, how spooked and baffled and disliked they are over so much of the world. Think of the harping on about the 'special relationship' – not so much special, as the only one possible for two such done-up wallflowers. Surely, apart from anything else, with more language-learning, there would have been fewer wars over the past decades?

Appeal to emotion (pathos).

On the individual level, think of the loss of possibility, the preordained narrowness of a life encased in one language, as if you were only ever allowed one, as if it were your skin in which you were born. Or your cage. That's your lot. When the great Australian poet Les Murray said: 'We are a language species', he didn't mean English. We think and are and have our being in, and in and out of languages – and where's the joy and the richness, if you don't even have two to rub together? If you don't have another language, you are condemned to occupy the same positions, the same phrases, all your life.

Another way of engaging with texts is through note taking. One method of organizing your notes is by using the Cornell Note-taking System, originally developed in the 1940s by Walter Pauk of Cornell University. A very basic template for Cornell Notes looks like this:

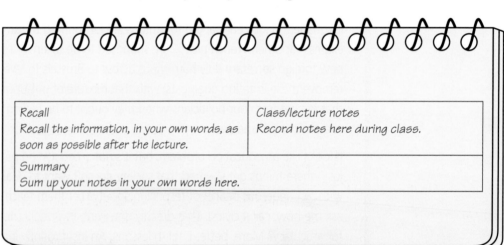

Recall	Class/lecture notes
Recall the information, in your own words, as soon as possible after the lecture.	Record notes here during class.
Summary	
Sum up your notes in your own words here.	

While this method may work best for more content-based subjects such as history or biology, it can easily be adapted to work for English Language and Literature. Consider the following as an example of how to format your notes on a text:

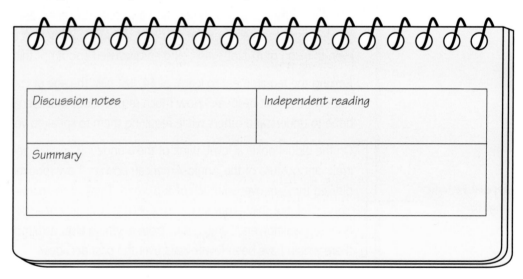

Discussion notes	Independent reading
Summary	

Instead of focusing the largest column on class notes, you could jot down your ideas while reading the text independently. What features do you notice? What questions arise? The left-hand column could be devoted to notes you take during class discussions on the text. Perhaps a classmate makes an interesting observation or inspires you to consider a text from a different point of view. Finally, the summary section could be a place for you to synthesize your independent notes with those you have taken during class.

Alternatively, you could format your notes using a three-column approach, as in the example below:

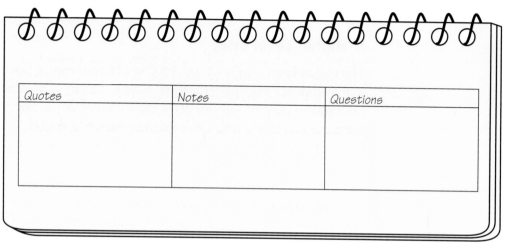

It is worth noting that there are many apps available which make electronic note taking simple and straightforward. Research supports handwritten notes as the most effective way of remembering information, but you will need to find a method which works for you. As with annotation, there is no right or wrong way to take notes, but you will gain much more from note taking if you establish some sort of structure to your notes rather than randomly listing your observations as you read.

Assessment overview

Textual analysis is a key element of the Language A: Language and Literature course, and it features in each of the assessments, some more explicitly than others. Each of the assessment tasks shares a common assessment criterion — analysis and evaluation — which focuses on your ability to demonstrate how textual features and authorial choices shape meaning.

▇ Paper 1

Paper 1 assesses your ability to independently analyse unseen texts under timed conditions. You will have 1 hour and 15 minutes at Standard Level (SL) or 2 hours and 15 minutes at Higher Level (HL) to write a guided textual analysis on one (SL) or two (HL) unseen (non-literary) texts. The texts will include guiding questions which will suggest a stylistic point of entry into each text. You are not expected to produce a fully-fledged guided textual analysis on all aspects of the text, but rather a more focused reading of the text or texts.

You will develop your skills in textual analysis throughout the Language A: Language and Literature course. Paper 1 is not connected to any one particular area of study, but is a holistic assessment of your ability to demonstrate an appreciation of how language and style shape meaning, which is one of the main aims of the course.

■ Paper 2

In Paper 2, you are required to compare and contrast two of the literary works you have studied in connection with one of a choice of four questions. Because you will not have access to the works that you choose to write about during the exam, you will not be expected to demonstrate the same level of close reading that you will for Paper 1. Your analysis may be broader in nature, as opposed to being focused on the specific language of the works, but you will still have to analyse certain aspects of the works, in relation to your chosen question. The International Baccalaureate Organization guide recommends preparing three works for the paper in conjunction and consultation with your teacher.

■ Higher Level essay

The Higher Level essay is a 1 200–1 500 word formal essay, following a line of inquiry of your own choice into one of the texts studied – literary or non-literary. You may choose to focus your inquiry through one of the critical lenses, or you may choose a specific literary feature such as characterization, narrative structure or symbol.

■ Individual oral

The internal assessment component of the course consists of a 15-minute individual oral (IO) exploring two of the texts (one literary and one non-literary) in relation to a global issue of your choice. The first ten minutes consists of your analysis of a chosen extract or extracts and the overall texts in connection with the chosen global issue. In the remaining five minutes, the teacher will ask you questions that will encourage further development, exploration or discussion. Many of the close-reading skills that you will have to demonstrate for Paper 1 will also be demonstrated here in the IO.

■ Learner portfolio

Although the learner portfolio (LP) is not formally assessed by the IB, it is a central element of the course and is instrumental in the preparation of all assessment components. The LP is a collection and selection of your work, including all sorts of tasks you might develop in your interaction with the texts and in your preparation of all assessment components. It consists not only of entries where you reflect on the texts studied, but also of all sorts of activities which you might engage in as you respond critically or creatively to the texts you read. This could include annotations, notes or other activities which show your active engagement with the texts. The LP can be paper, electronic or multi-modal.

Textual analysis and the approaches to learning

Throughout your Language A: Language and Literature course of study, you will have the opportunity to develop many of the approaches to learning (ATL) skills – both in and outside the classroom – in group and individual settings. Through the process of textual analysis, you will specifically develop your critical thinking and creative thinking skills, as outlined on the next page.

Critical thinking skills	**How can students think critically?**
	Gather and organize relevant information to formulate an argument.
	Evaluate evidence and arguments.
	Draw reasonable conclusions and generalizations.
	Consider ideas from multiple perspectives.
	Develop contrary or opposing arguments.
Creative thinking skills	**How can students be creative?**
	Generate novel ideas and consider new perspectives.
	Make unexpected or unusual connections between objects and/ or ideas.
	Create original works and ideas; use existing works and ideas in new ways.
	Generate metaphors and analogies.

Conclusion

You may think that this book is only useful within the context of your English studies. However, the practice of textual analysis can have many wider-reaching benefits. Developing your analytical skills can increase your vocabulary, improve your verbal skills, critical thinking skills and memory function, encourage you to develop empathy and engagement with other art forms and help you become a better writer yourself.

The remaining chapters in this book will help you develop specific skills for interpreting different text types, as well as for writing about those text types for your IB assessments.

Works cited

Hofmann, Michael, 'To speak another language isn't just cultured, it's a blow against stupidity', *The Guardian*, 15 August 2010, Web, accessed 2 January 2019, **www.theguardian.com/ commentisfree/2010/aug/15/michael-hofmann-learn-another-language**

International Baccalaureate Organization, *Language A: Language and Literature guide*. Cardiff, 2011.

International Baccalaureate Organization, *Language A: Language and Literature guide*. Cardiff, 2019.

2 | Approaches to non-literary texts

You will examine a wide variety of texts, both literary and non-literary, throughout your Language A: Language and Literature course. Literary works can generally be grouped into four main forms: poetry, prose fiction, prose non-fiction and drama. Non-literary texts, however, are categorized by *text type*, of which there are a seemingly infinite number. If the definition of a text is 'anything from which information can be extracted', then we are encountering – and arguably creating – texts all the time in our daily lives.

Some texts can be considered literary forms, usually within the non-fiction category (for example, biography, diary, essay, memoir, travel writing). You may indeed focus on a series of letters or a pastiche within your study of literature. However, when studied as a single work (and especially in the context of developing your skills in unseen textual analysis), these text types will be treated as non-literary.

You will not be expected to study a prescribed number or type of non-literary texts within the language component of your IB English course of study (the literature component is more prescribed, with a minimum of four works required at Standard Level and six works at Higher Level; the syllabus should include a balance of works in terms of period, place, gender of the author, and literary form), nor will you be expected to learn the features or characteristics of all possible text types. The skills of analysing one text type can be transferable to another.

The rest of this chapter will guide you through the analysis of many of the key aspects of non-literary texts. It is important not to view these elements in isolation, but to consider how they work together to achieve a specific purpose. The activities will each focus on a specific element, but it is impossible to consider one element without taking into account others; therefore, it might be a good idea to skim the chapter before engaging in the activities. Additionally, we do not want to suggest that you should adopt a linear approach to analysing a text; you may find that tone is the first thing that jumps out at you, or you may be attuned to picking up on figurative language as you read. The purpose of these exercises is to give you the tools to analyse with more confidence, not to suggest a one-size-fits-all approach.

Content

An initial reading of any text should focus on **content**. Only once you have grasped the literal meaning of the text can you begin to consider other layers of meaning. If you start by developing a solid understanding of the content of the text (the *what*), then you will be able to work towards a more nuanced understanding of the style of the text (the *how* and *why*). Jumping in to an analysis of style first will only demonstrate a lack of foundational knowledge.

■ Author's message

As you examine the content of a text, you need to ask yourself what the author's message is. This is not necessarily the same thing as the purpose of the text, which will be explored in more detail later in the chapter. The central message is related to larger themes that the text reflects.

The following extract from Elizabeth Gilbert's travel memoir *Eat Pray Love* is a good example of a text with a central message that is distinct from its purpose.

■ Example: *Eat Pray Love* by Elizabeth Gilbert

I've never had less of a plan in my life than I do upon arrival in Bali. In all my history of careless travels, this is the most carelessly I've ever landed anyplace. I don't know where I'm going to live, I don't know what I'm going to do, I don't know what the exchange rate is, I don't know how to get a taxi at the airport or even where to ask

5 that taxi to take me. Nobody is expecting my arrival. I have no friends in Indonesia, or even friends-of-friends. And here's the problem about traveling with an out-of-date guidebook, and then not reading it anyway: I didn't realize that I'm actually not allowed to stay in Indonesia for four months, even if I want to. I find this out only upon entry into the country. Turns out I'm allowed only a one-month tourist visa. It

10 hadn't occurred to me that the Indonesian government would be anything less than delighted to host me in their country for just as long as I pleased to stay.

As the nice immigration official is stamping my passport with permission to stay in Bali for only and exactly thirty days, I ask him in my most friendly manner if I can please remain longer.

15 'No,' he says, in his most friendly manner. The Balinese are most famously friendly.

'See, I'm supposed to stay here for three or four months,' I tell him.

I don't mention that it is a prophecy that my staying here for three or four months was predicted by an elderly and quite possibly demented Balinese medicine man, during a ten-minute palm-reading. I'm not sure how to explain this.

20 But what did that medicine man tell me, now that I think of it? Did he actually say that I would come back to Bali and spend three or four months living with him? Did he really say 'living with' him? Or did he just want me to drop by again sometime if I was in the neighborhood and give him another ten bucks for another palm-reading? Did he say I would come back, or that I should come back? Did he really say, 'See

25 you later, alligator'? Or was it, 'In a while, crocodile'?

I haven't had any communication with the medicine man since that one evening. I wouldn't know how to contact him, anyway. What might his address be? 'Medicine Man, On His Porch, Bali, Indonesia'? I don't know whether he's dead or alive. I remember that he seemed exceedingly old two years ago when we met; anything

30 could have happened to him since then. All I have for sure is his name Ketut Liyer and the memory that he lives in a village just outside the town of Ubud. But I don't remember the name of the village.

Maybe I should have thought all this through better.

The purpose of this piece is primarily to entertain. This purpose is conveyed through a range of techniques characteristic of travel writing. These are listed in the Travel writing techniques box on the next page and can be applied or adapted to other pieces of travel writing that you may encounter. Further conventions of text type are covered in more detail in the Style and Structure sections on pages 23 and 34.

KEY TERM

First-person
narration – the
author/narrator
as an active
participant in the
experience he or
she is sharing, not
a passive observer.

TRAVEL WRITING TECHNIQUES

✔ **First-person narration**: the author/narrator is an active participant in the experience he or she is sharing, not a passive observer.

✔ **Focus on a key event/experience**: good travel writing is not a catalogue of every detail from the author's journey, but rather a focused account of a specific moment or series of moments with a central message or theme.

✔ **Appealing to the senses**: travel writers use sensory imagery to immerse the reader in the experience.

✔ **Use of humour and anecdotes:** travel writers often use humour and quirky anecdotes to engage the audience.

✔ **A mix of narration and reflection:** a mixture of in-the-moment descriptions and retrospective reflection. Travel writing, especially of the literary kind, often ends with a lesson or message to the reader.

✔ **Use of descriptive details**: the setting is described in detail so that readers feel as if they are there. In more *literary* travel writing, writers also include descriptions of people in the same way that novelists characterize people in their stories. Good travel writers do this with sensitivity, avoiding stereotypes. (We do not really see this feature illustrated in this particular extract, but it is worth noting that it is present in the work as a whole.) Travel writing will also include literary elements such as dialogue, metaphor, hyperbole, etc.

The central message of the text, however, is perhaps more subjective. One possible interpretation of this particular extract could be that Gilbert wishes to express the idea that some of the most significant experiences in life happen spontaneously. This idea is reflected in the way she characterizes herself as impulsive, or 'careless'; she hasn't fully prepared for this part of her journey, having based her decision to go to Bali only on the medicine man's 'prophecy'. Or we could say that some events or experiences which may seem insignificant in the moment take on greater significance when we have the ability to reflect on them at a later time. There is nothing in the extract to directly suggest this theme; however, the fact that she has included it in her memoir (and in such detail) indicates that it was a significant moment in her journey.

■ Tone and mood

Another aspect of a text which you will notice during an initial reading is tone and mood. Tone is the attitude of the writer or speaker towards his or her subject. Mood is the feeling that is evoked in the reader (or audience) as a result of the tone that is set. In literature, mood is often referred to as atmosphere; in a non-literary text, we can consider mood more like a state of mind.

Tone and mood are conveyed through language, so as you move towards a deeper level of understanding you will need to consider what – and how – specific elements of style shape the tone and mood of a text.

When describing tone and mood, it is important to use specific, precise adjectives. A text may appear to have a casual style, but you would not necessarily say that it has a casual tone; *casual* is a bit too vague. On the next page are some examples of words that you could use to characterize tone and mood. These lists are by no means exhaustive; you may indeed be able to think of many more words to add to this list. Some words may also be applicable to both tone and mood.

Tone words	Mood words
Aggressive	Bittersweet
Angry	Bleak
Attached/detached	Cheerful
Bitter	Confident
Compassionate	Content
Encouraging	Disappointed
Friendly	Eerie
Gory	Enraged
Haunting	Furious
Humorous	Gloomy
Innocent	Hopeless
Mysterious	Idyllic
Nonchalant	Indolent
Playful	Inspired
Poignant	Motivated
Serious	Relaxed
Suspenseful	Relieved
Sympathetic	Satisfied
Tasteful/distasteful	Tense
Tender	Uncertain
Witty	

■ The tone of a tweet

Social media texts, such as blogs and tweets, are useful for exploring tone and mood. With immediate, unfiltered access to a global audience, these text types are often characterized by a casual, conversational style. Their interactive nature almost encourages this style, with fellow users replying and re-tweeting to voice their approval or disapproval, or simply to carry on with the conversation.

Tweets, in particular, reflect a very distinctive tone. With only a limited number of characters at one's disposal, the author of a tweet must pay careful consideration to word choice (diction), sentence structure, punctuation and **syntax** to convey the intended attitude. President Donald Trump is one of the most famous Twitter users to date since the platform's release in 2006. Trump's tweets are often designed to provoke an emotional response in the audience – in both his followers and his critics – like the one here which you can access at **https://bit.ly/2FHxn92**.

Your description of Trump's tone in this example might be dependent on your political views (more on this later when we explore context), but whether you characterize his tone as angry or authoritative, the language is there to support you:

■ Use of capital letters, which is meant to imitate shouting ('NOT', 'WALL').

■ Emotive diction used to characterize migrants as a threat to America ('stone cold criminals').

■ Repetitive use of imperatives to reinforce the urgency of his message ('Do it by plane, do it by bus, do it anyway you want …').

■ Direct address/call to action ('Congress, fund the WALL!').

KEY TERM

Syntax – the arrangement of words in a sentence or text.

■ Tone and bias

KEY TERM

Bias – unbalanced language that suggests support for a particular ideological view and/or group of people.

One important consideration when exploring tone is whether or not you detect any biases. **Bias** is defined as language which is unbalanced; that is, language which suggests support for a particular ideological view and/or group of people. Bias can be overt or it can be more subtle. You can detect bias by looking for certain techniques and asking yourself the questions shown in the box below.

DETECTING BIAS

- ✔ What type of publication does the text appear in? What is its reputation? Does it appeal to a particular audience in terms of age, level of education, political views, etc? (This might take some wider research.)
- ✔ What sources are quoted? What are their credentials or qualifications? In other words, how can you tell that they are credible?
- ✔ What evidence is presented?
- ✔ What's missing? Are you left with any questions? Does it appear that anything has been deliberately left out?
- ✔ Do you notice any *loaded language* (eg, emotive language or words with a particularly negative or positive connotation)?

ACTIVITY 1: DETECTING BIAS

Read the following two news reports, based on the same story and published on the same day via the QR codes on the left. Consider how each text presents the information. Use the questions above to detect if there is any bias. The first article is from the Mail Online headlined 'Caravan of migrants swells to 7,000 and stretches more than a mile long...' and the second article is from The Guardian headlined 'Desperate Central American refugees cross into Mexico from river'.

Context

Context refers to the circumstances that surround a text – all of the external factors which are needed to fully understand the text itself. Some critics argue that literary works should be judged on their artistic qualities alone. While this may work in certain cases and for certain texts, most non-literary texts cannot be fully understood or appreciated without some knowledge of the contexts in which they were produced and/or received.

It is important to note that when examining unseen texts you may not always have access to contextual details. While you may be able to infer some elements of time, place and culture from the text itself, you should avoid making unfounded assumptions or generalizations. When studying texts independently or within the classroom setting, it is important to read *around* the text to develop a contextual understanding relevant to your interpretation.

■ Time and place

It is important to consider both the time and place in which a piece was produced as well as, in the case of a work of fiction, when it was set. What is the historical backdrop? What was the political, social or economic environment of the time/place? What cultural or religious customs are reflective of the age?

■ Example: 'March for Our Lives' speech

The power of Emma Gonzalez's 'March for Our Lives' speech, delivered on 24 March 2018 in response to the mass shooting at Marjorie Stoneman Douglas High School in Parkland, Florida just over a month earlier, can only really be understood in the context of the wider debate surrounding gun control in the United States. Her message was all the more emotive – for people on both sides of the issue – because of the political climate at that time. You can access the speech at **https://bit.ly/2I6RBFB**.

ACTIVITY 2: CONSIDERING HISTORICAL CONTEXT

Read the following letter from Wilfred Owen to his mother and consider what historical elements you would need to be familiar with in order to fully appreciate the letter's emotional impact.

To Susan Owen

Thurs. 31 October [1918] 6:15 p.m.

[2nd Manchester Regt.]

Dearest Mother,

I will call the place from which I'm now writing 'The Smoky Cellar of the Forester's House'. I write on the first sheet of the writing pad which came in the parcel yesterday. Luckily the parcel was small, as it reached me just before we moved off to the line. Thus only the paraffin was unwelcome in my pack. My servant & I ate the chocolate in the cold middle of last night, crouched under a draughty Tamboo, roofed with planks. I husband the Malted Milk for tonight, & tomorrow night. The handkerchief & socks are most opportune, as the ground is marshy*, & I have a slight cold!

So thick is the smoke in this cellar that I can hardly see by a candle 12 ins. away, and so thick are the inmates that I can hardly write for pokes, nudges & jolts. On my left the Coy. Commander snores on a bench: other officers repose on wire beds behind me. At my right hand, Kellett, a delightful servant of A Coy. in The Old Days radiates joy & contentment from pink cheeks and baby eyes. He laughs with a signaller, to whose left ear is glued the Receiver; but whose eyes rolling with gaiety show that he is listening with his right ear to a merry corporal, who appears at this distance away (some three feet) nothing [but] a gleam of white teeth & a wheeze of jokes.

Splashing my hand, an old soldier with a walrus moustache peels & drops potatoes into the pot. By him, Keyes, my cook, chops wood; another feeds the smoke with the damp wood.

It is a great life. I am more oblivious than alas! yourself, dear Mother, of the ghastly glimmering of the guns outside, & the hollow crashing of the shells.

There is no danger down here, or if any, it will be well over before you read these lines**.

I hope you are as warm as I am; as serene in your room as I am here; and that you think of me never in bed as resignedly as I think of you always in bed. Of this I am certain you could not be visited by a band of friends half so fine as surround me here.

Ever Wilfred x

Notes:

* The Ors Canal was some 70 feet wide bank to bank, except at the locks, with an average depth of 6–8 feet. All bridges had been demolished or prepared for demolition. Low ground on both sides of the canal had been inundated by the Germans; most of it was swamp. The Germans held the eastern bank.

** Strong patrolling continued till zero hour for the IX Corps attack, 5:45 a.m., 4 November. 14 Brigade crossed; 96 Brigade, which included 2nd Manchesters, was not successful. The engineers got a bridge across, but the area was swept with shell and machine-gun fire. Two platoons made the crossing, but the bridge was then destroyed. The remainder of the battalion crossed at Ors, where 1st Dorsets had secured a crossing. Wilfred Owen was killed on the canal bank on 4 November. One other officer (Second-Lieutenant Kirk, posthumously awarded the VC) and twenty-two other ranks were also killed; three officers and eighty-one other ranks were wounded; eighteen other ranks missing. A week later, the war was over.

Source: Harry Ransom Center/The Wilfred Owen Literary Estate via First World War Poetry Digital Archive

■ Audience and purpose

The audience of a literary work is, in general, quite broad. The genre or sub-genre may have some impact on the target audience; for example, historical fiction or psychological thrillers will appeal to readers with those specific interests. Mass market fiction does not generally target a specific demographic in terms of age, education level, political view, etc. Non-literary texts, on the other hand, usually have a much narrower audience, and this is determined by the text type. For example, a blog about vegan baking will appeal to individuals who have adopted a vegan diet and/or enjoy baking. A travel guide focused on budget travel in Thailand will most likely appeal to a younger (perhaps more adventurous) audience of a specific economic level.

The purpose of a text could be any of the following:

✓ To entertain

✓ To inform

✓ To persuade

✓ To advise

✓ To instruct

✓ To analyse

✓ To argue

✓ To explain

✓ To describe.

A literary work's primary purpose is aesthetic, but a non-literary text's purpose will, again, depend on the text type itself. For example, the purposes of the vegan baking blog and the budget travel guide might be to inform, explain or instruct. An opinion column will likely aim to persuade.

KEY TERM

Jargon – words that are used in a specific context that may be difficult to understand, often involving technical terminology.

When considering a text's audience and purpose, it is important to ask yourself how the language of the text is used to target the audience or how it reflects the text's central purpose. If we return again to the example of the vegan baking blog, the sentence structure is likely to be simple and the instructions very clear and straightforward. The vocabulary (diction) will also appeal to the audience: if the target audience is amateur, beginner bakers, then the language will likely be free of jargon. If, however, the target audience is more experienced bakers, then this would influence the amount of jargon or baking terminology that is used. This attention to language will help you avoid making unfounded generalizations and allow you to move beyond a superficial understanding of the text to a more sophisticated analysis.

A good example of a text with a very clear audience and purpose is shown in the following electronic text 'Swamp Water'.

Microscopy as a hobby or profession
Public Group, 4287 members

Swamp Water

Posted by: edwilli Sun Oct 24, 2004 9:51am

For almost a year now I have been following the behaviour of a variety of amoebas and flagellates in a 20 cm diameter crystallization dish half full of gunk (and topped up from time to time with distilled water) taken from the swamp on our property …

The first interesting micro-organisms to draw my attention were amoeboid flagellates of the genus Naegleria. No proof of this identification is offered, but I did spend a couple of years investigating them in South Africa long ago. Now and again a few grains of rice are dropped in around the edges. At one stage a few dozen small nematodes hatched and were to be seen crawling up the glass. They died down after a while but probably bred and there may be eggs ready to hatch later …

Soon after the slide is prepared large numbers of sulphur bacteria (coiled, one turn, with numerous granules) are to be found in close proximity to the Vaseline* seal. There are also helical organisms large and small. One had escaped notice because of its minute size and has now been tentatively identified as Leptospira biflexa. They also proliferate at a rapid rate, also close to the Vaseline, and can be found in large numbers clustered round encysted amoebae. This particular Spirochete is very easy to culture and all it needs is fatty acids and a few vitamins.

The Vaseline is a very important part of this micro-environment, not only as a nutrient. Many small bays and completely enclosed chambers are formed in which, sometimes, almost pure 'cultures' of some bacteria appear. Isolated as they are from the rest of the chamber they are very interesting to watch. Sometimes these little chambers become completely filled with cells and population density halts further growth.

These micro-environments, that seem to go on indefinitely, make it very easy to understand the fascination of the early microscopists who must have been amazed, if not shocked and horrified by what they saw in their water samples. But I doubt many kept the slides for long. I have some that are at least nine months old and still going strong … These preparations are fascinating and keep me busy when I'm not building contraptions for the microscope, such as electronic flashes and Halogen lamp holders. I have become as enthusiastic, mainly due to interaction with members of this group, as I was when using my own beautiful Zeiss Winkel** (mainly on bovine blood slides) at the tender age of 21 in Rhodesia.

*Vaseline: brand of petroleum jelly

**Zeiss Winkel: brand of microscope

↩ Reply

We immediately recognise that the text is a post on the message board of a group page for individuals interested in microscopy as a hobby or profession. The medium (a post to the World Wide Web) may suggest a broad audience. However, we can see from the heading that the group consists of fewer than 5000 members, which narrows the audience to a specific number of people within this particular online community. The author of the message uses scientific terminology and jargon familiar to professional microscopists (eg, 'amoeboid flagellates', 'helical organisms', 'my own beautiful Zeiss Winkel'), but the reflective, almost conversational tone appeals to the hobbyists in the group as well. The nature of the text as a post on a message board suggests that the audience is engaged and can interact with the person posting, as emphasized by the 'Reply' button at the bottom of the message. The author's purpose is to describe his observations. His final comment sums up his motivation for sharing his experience with a community of like-minded individuals: 'I have become as enthusiastic, mainly due to interaction with members of this group, as I was when using my own beautiful Zeiss Winkel (mainly on bovine blood slides) at the tender age of 21 in Rhodesia.'

ACTIVITY 3: CONSIDERING TARGET AUDIENCE

Examine the following text and consider the target audience. In what ways do the layout and design of this web page engage younger readers?

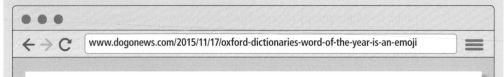

www.dogonews.com/2015/11/17/oxford-dictionaries-word-of-the-year-is-an-emoji

DOGOnews
ELA-Science-Social Studies

NEWS BOOKS MOVIES   SEARCH   KIDS TEACHERS SIGN IN

CURRENT EVENTS | SCIENCE | SOCIAL STUDIES | WORLD | ENVIRONMENT | FUN | VIDEO | SPORTS

Oxford Dictionaries 'Word Of The Year' Is ... An Emoji?

By Meera Dolasia on November 17, 2015

We all know that life without emojis, (*the small digital icons that we use* **ad nauseam**) would be extremely boring. Hence, it is only fitting that the editors of the **prestigious** Oxford English Dictionary chose – The emoji with the tears of joy as its "Word of the Year" for 2015.

The company that announced its unusual word choice on November 16th said that it was picked over several other traditional **contenders**. Among them were "**refugee**", "**sharing economy**" and "**on fleek**". However, it was this simple emoji that **resonated** with the editors because it appeared to best describe the "**ethos**, mood, and preoccupations of 2015."

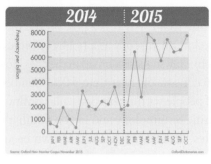

They also thought that this was a good year to pay **homage** to the emoji. For though they have been around since the late 1990s, the use of the digital icons and the word that describes them, has escalated sharply this year. Besides, emojis are now used by people of all ages, not just teenagers.

Also, though the word stems from the Japanese language – e (*picture*), moji (*character or letter*), the digital icons can be understood by everyone regardless of the language they speak. Hence it only makes sense to acknowledge their importance to global communication.

As to how they selected from the thousands of emojis that are available? The company says that they partnered with a leading mobile technology company SwiftKey to determine the most popular emoji. Turns out that "tears of joy" is the most used icon. According to SwiftKey, made up 17% of all emojis used in the U.S.A and an **astounding** 20% in the **United Kingdom**!

Though this is the first time the Oxford University Press has selected an image for its "word of the year", it is not the first time they have tried to **incorporate** modern **lingo** into their 150-year-old publication. In 2013, in **recognition** of the growing popularity of self-portraits, the editors selected "selfie", for the "Word of the Year"!

Listen to Article

Generate citations in MLA, APA & Chicago formats for this article.

Vocabulary   Play Game

ad nauseam   astounding   contenders   ethos   homage   incorporate   lingo   on fleek
prestigious   recognition   refugee   resonated   sharing economy

Geography

United Kingdom!

Sign In or Sign Up
for unlimited access to Assignments

■ Context of interpretation

The context of production refers to the author's circumstances at the time of writing or composing a text. The context of *interpretation* is about the reader's (or audience's) circumstances, and this is ever-changing. For example, audience perceptions of 1950s advertisements, like the ones shown below, for cleaning products have changed significantly since their production. These products were initially targeted at housewives, but the images used to reflect the target audience are now generally seen as sexist by Western audiences.

Each individual reader will approach a text with his or her own set of circumstances related to gender, ethnicity, culture, religion, class, level of education, political affiliation and so on, and each of these circumstances influences our reading of a text. This makes the context of interpretation a very personal layer of the text.

ACTIVITY 4: INTERPRETING PROPAGANDA

The following text is a US army recruitment poster from the First World War. How do you think a modern audience would react to the messages conveyed in the text? Note that we will cover how to analyse visual texts in Chapter 4, including how to develop a visual vocabulary, so your response here does not have to include specific terminology.

Style

Hopefully by now you will have noticed that there is a great deal of overlap between the different layers of a text. In fact, it would be nearly impossible to consider content and context without also giving some consideration to style. If you focus on any of these elements in isolation, you will not be able to demonstrate beyond a superficial level of understanding on your IB assessments.

Style is the *how* of a text, and the assessment criteria for Paper 1 makes explicit reference to that word:

> To what extent does the candidate analyse and evaluate *how* textual features and/or authorial choices shape meaning?

Merely identifying the stylistic features of a text will not allow you to demonstrate a very sophisticated level of analysis and evaluation of the text. We will explore how to achieve this in writing in Chapter 5.

KEY TERMS

Literary device – a technique or tool that a writer uses to create an effect; examples include imagery and personification.

Allusion – a reference to something without a literal or explicit mention of it.

Hyperbole – exaggeration to make a situation seem more dramatic or humorous.

Register – the level of formality in writing or speaking.

You may be used to referring to the tools that an author uses as **literary devices**. It is true that certain devices may be unique to literary works; however, many non-literary texts will contain such devices. For example, an advertisement may include metaphors or sound devices. A speech may include **allusions** or **hyperbole**. A more precise term to use when referring to the devices that are present in any text, literary or non-literary, is stylistic devices. We will focus here on those elements of style which are most common in non-literary texts.

■ Register

Register refers to the level of formality in writing or speaking. Certain text types are characterized by a more formal register, while others are more informal, as we will see in the example and activity that follow. Register is achieved by carefully considering word choice and sentence structures.

■ Diction

When we refer to word choice, we are talking about diction. Diction can be broken down into different categories, some of which are outlined below. It is important when writing about diction to identify the specific aspect of diction you are referring to; this precision will allow you to demonstrate greater knowledge and appreciation of language.

- **Vocabulary:** specific vocabulary reflects a particular style. For example, multisyllabic Latin-based words versus shorter, punchier Anglo-Saxon words would suggest a more formal, elevated style. The use of jargon, slang or colloquialisms might also reveal certain things about the speaker's personality.

- **Denotation vs connotation:** words have both denotative (literal) and connotative (emotional) meanings. The word *home* is a good example of a word that has both a denotative and a connotative meaning. Literally, a home is a place where one lives, but emotionally the word can conjure up feelings of comfort, family and security.

- **Concrete vs abstract words:** concrete language refers to things that we can physically observe (eg, table, book, sky). Abstract language refers to intangible ideas like love, truth, sadness, etc.

- **Figurative language:** the choice to use direct language or to reveal emotions more subtly through figurative language is another important tool at the writer's disposal. Different types of figurative language will be explored in more detail in Chapter 3.

■ Syntax

Syntax refers to the rules and principles governing sentence structure and word order. When analysing a text's level of formality, you would examine aspects such as sentence type (simple, compound, complex, compound-complex) and the order of words, phrases and clauses.

■ Voice

Verbs are characterized as having either active or passive voice, and this is a key element of style. You may have been told to avoid using passive voice; this can be a good general rule to follow, but passive voice can be used to achieve a certain effect. For example, if the *do-er* of the action (the subject) is unknown, unwanted or unneeded in the sentence, then the passive voice may be the more appropriate choice. Likewise, the writer may wish to emphasize the action in the sentence, or simply use the passive voice for sentence variety. Whatever the reason, writers should be aware of why they are using passive voice – and be wary of its overuse.

KEY TERM

Rhetorical question – a question that implies an answer, which is a subtle way of persuading someone or influencing someone's opinion.

Sentence types, sometimes also referred to as modes, can also reflect a specific authorial *voice*. Overuse of exclamatory sentences, for example, can reflect an informal register. The four main types of sentence include: declarative (statement), interrogative (question), exclamatory (exclamation) and imperative (command). Some sentence types are characteristic of certain text types. For example, an information leaflet will most likely include more declarative sentences; a set of instructions will include mainly imperatives; and a speech is likely to include more interrogative sentences in the form of **rhetorical questions**.

■ Essays

An essay is broadly defined as a non-fiction text which develops an argument. There are several different types of essay, including – but not limited to – expository, persuasive, narrative and personal. The subject matter, purpose, audience and length may vary from essay to essay, but most essays will share one key feature: a formal register (often referred to as an *academic* register). We can see this in an extract from Virginia Woolf's essay 'The Art of Biography'.

■ Example: 'The Art of Biography' by Virginia Woolf

The art of biography, we say — but at once go on to ask, is biography an art? The question is foolish perhaps, and ungenerous certainly, considering the keen pleasure that biographers have given us. But the question asks itself so often that there must be something behind it. There it is, whenever a new biography is opened, casting
5 its shadow on the page; and there would seem to be something deadly in that shadow, for after all, of the multitude of lives that are written, how few survive!

But the reason for this high death rate, the biographer might argue, is that biography, compared with the arts of poetry and fiction, is a young art. Interest in our selves and in other people's selves is a late development of the human mind.
10 Not until the eighteenth century in England did that curiosity express itself in writing the lives of private people. Only in the nineteenth century was biography fully grown and hugely prolific. If it is true that there have been only three great biographers— Johnson, Boswell, and Lockhart—the reason, he argues, is that the time was short; and his plea, that the art of biography has had but little time to establish itself
15 and develop itself, is certainly borne out by the textbooks. Tempting as it is to explore the reason—why, that is, the self that writes a book of prose came into being so many centuries after the self that writes a poem, why Chaucer preceded Henry James—it is better to leave that insoluble question unasked, and so pass to his next reason for the lack of masterpieces. It is that the art of biography is
20 the most restricted of all the arts. He has his proof ready to hand. Here it is in the preface in which Smith, who has written the life of Jones, takes this opportunity of thanking old friends who have lent letters, and 'last but not least' Mrs. Jones, the widow, for that help 'without which,' as he puts it, 'this biography could not have been written.' Now the novelist, he points out, simply says in his foreword, 'Every
25 character in this book is fictitious.' The novelist is free; the biographer is tied.

There, perhaps, we come within hailing distance of that very difficult, again perhaps insoluble, question: What do we mean by calling a book a work of art? At any rate,

here is a distinction between biography and fiction—a proof that they differ in the very stuff of which they are made. One is made with the help of friends, of facts; the other
30 is created without any restrictions save those that the artist, for reasons that seem good to him, chooses to obey. That is a distinction; and there is good reason to think that in the past biographers have found it not only a distinction but a very cruel distinction.

Woolf's vocabulary is elevated ('considering the keen pleasure', 'within hailing distance', 'insoluble') – as you would expect from an academic essay. There are no instances in which she uses abbreviations or contractions. Woolf's authorial voice is objective and she uses a variety of sentence types, employing the dash frequently to add qualifying statements or interject parenthetical thoughts into her main points. This element of style reflects a complex level of thought, which echoes the complexity of the argument itself. Although Woolf does use a couple of rhetorical questions and one exclamation, she generally adheres to declarative sentences, most of which are complex in nature; there is a refined, confident and assured tone reflected in the language.

■ Blogs

A blog is a rather indistinct text type in the sense that it may or may not have a clearly defined audience (after all, blogs are accessible to anyone who has access to the internet), and the purpose could range from instructive or informative to purely entertaining. Many blogs can read like essays, and like an essay, a blog may make an argument. Whatever the subject matter of a blog, its register tends to be less formal. It could be considered a sort of conversation between the author and their readers, like a public diary.

ACTIVITY 5: COMPARING REGISTERS

Read the following blog post, from author Meg Gardiner's blog *Lying for a Living*. How does this post compare with Woolf's essay? What elements of language reflect an informal register?

https://meggardiner.wordpress.com/2006/07/27/hello-world/

It's alive

Posted on July 27, 2006

10 Comments

'I like to read about things that are real.'

My friend looked away as he said that to me. He felt embarrassed because my new novel was sitting untouched on his desk. He felt compelled to explain why he hadn't opened it. He doesn't read fiction, not unless it's jammed down his throat.

I didn't object. Number one, he had bought the book, with actual cash. Two, he was cooking dinner for me and my family. Three, I don't jam things down people's throats except on the page, and then generally only if the character deserves it. But my friend was wrong.

Love, death, anger, greed, envy, and crazy people running amok in California. That's what's in my books. What's not real?

Yes, I know it's all my own invention. But there's something real in storytelling, which is why, despite the name of this blog, I don't consider fiction a lie. It's true, and it's alive. And that's one of the things I'll be talking about here.

KEY TERMS

Appeal – a persuasive technique split into three types: ethos, logos and pathos.

Ethos – an ethical appeal to the authority of the writer or speaker.

Logos – an appeal to logic.

Pathos – an appeal to emotion.

■ Persuasive language

Persuasive language is all around us. We are constantly influenced by the language of advertisements, political campaigns, charity appeals, newspaper opinion pieces and other such texts.

Persuasion relies on appeals to the audience. There are three types of **appeal**: the ethical appeal (**ethos**), the logical appeal (**logos**) and the emotional appeal (**pathos**).

Ethos is an appeal to the authority of the writer or speaker. Ethos involves building a sense of trust within the audience. This can be achieved in different ways by:

- sharing one's professional knowledge or personal experience
- relying on expert support
- adopting a formal, objective register (except, perhaps, when sharing personal experience)
- creating a *bond* with the audience (eg, by directly addressing the audience or making imperative commands to the audience, using inclusive language and personal pronouns like *you* and *we*).

Logos is an appeal to logic and is achieved by using logical, evidence-based support for one's argument. Evidence can include:

- facts and figures
- examples
- expert testimony.

Pathos is an appeal to emotion. Writers and speakers can stir emotions through diction and figurative language. In particular, the use of words with strong connotative meanings can trigger a range of emotions in an audience.

The most effective arguments use a combination of all three appeals. For example, an argument which is purely based on emotion would most likely be considered weak. Equally, an argument which is devoid of emotion, relying instead only on facts and statistics, would seem cold.

■ Example: Yemen Crisis Appeal

Appeals are persuasive techniques, but an *appeal* is also a specific text type, often used by charities and non-profit organizations. The following text is from Oxfam's Yemen Crisis Appeal. We will only examine the first part of the appeal here, but you can view the whole appeal on the Oxfam website at **https://bit.ly/1CYti6W** and see further examples of persuasive techniques at work.

Yemen Crisis Appeal

Continuing conflict, airstrikes and restrictions on imports have left 14 million people facing famine in Yemen.

Nearly half of all children aged between six months and five years are chronically malnourished.

Oxfam has reached more than 3 million people with lifesaving essentials, like clean water and cash to buy food - but the military onslaught around the port city of Hudaydah is putting yet more children, women and men at risk.

You can help.

Donate to Oxfam's Yemen response

Every report from our own staff and news teams on the ground brings harrowing accounts of families facing agonising hunger and suffering.

We can see several persuasive devices in just this short extract from the appeal. Perhaps the most dominant technique is pathos. The use of the colour red, for example, highlights the critical nature of the crisis. The dominant image of the malnourished child evokes an emotional response; the audience may feel pity or helplessness – feelings which may lead to action. The layout of the page, with the 'Donate to Oxfam's Yemen response' link positioned next to the image's caption, calls one to action: the link physically looks like an arrow, pointing towards the child in need. Logos is established in the main text through the use of facts and statistics. Ethos is also established in the third paragraph; the text highlights the work that Oxfam has already done to help with the crisis, showcasing its reputation for humanitarian aid. This is a good example of the three appeals working together to achieve the text's main purpose.

■ Other persuasive techniques

Other persuasive techniques include:

- **Rhetorical questions**: imply an answer, which is a subtle way of persuading someone or influencing someone's opinion.

- **Repetition**: the repeated use of a word, phrase or image draws attention to it and can therefore be an effective persuasive technique.

- **Enumeration (lists)**: listing creates a cumulative effect. For example, if an advertisement includes a list of all of the benefits of a particular product or service, then the audience (the potential consumer) is more likely to be persuaded of its use.

- **Triples ('the rule of three')**: this technique is essentially a type of enumeration. It is almost universally agreed that three is the magic number.

- **Hyperbole**: the use of exaggeration can make a situation seem more dramatic or humorous. Advertisers, for example, may exaggerate the need for an item. Political speakers may exaggerate the impact of a decision or event. The use of understatement, which is the opposite of hyperbole, can be equally effective in persuading an audience.

■ Propaganda and persuasion

Propaganda is a form of persuasion. The aim of propaganda is to promote a political cause or ideology through the use of information which is often biased or misleading. Propaganda can take many forms, such as advertisements, news reports, political cartoons (which we will examine in more detail in Chapter 4) or speeches. Many propaganda texts (including the recruitment poster you examined earlier in the section

KEY TERM

Propaganda – information presented in a biased way to influence the reader, often to promote a cause or ideology.

on context on page 23) use some of the same persuasive devices that have been outlined above. In fact, the line between persuasion and propaganda is a very thin one, and there is some debate over whether or not all forms of persuasion can be considered propaganda. Aaron Delwiche, in his article 'Propaganda Is Everywhere' on the *Propaganda Critic* website, has an interesting way of defining propaganda's influence:

> Propaganda can be as blatant as a swastika or as subtle as a joke. Its persuasive techniques are regularly applied by politicians, advertisers, journalists, radio personalities, and others who are interested in influencing human behavior. Propaganda can be used to accomplish positive social ends, as in campaigns to reduce drunk driving, but it is also used to win elections and to sell malt liquor (Concepts, and Everywhere).

Propaganda relies on specific techniques, the most common of which are outlined here:

- **Name-calling**: a technique whereby a person or idea is linked to a negative symbol.
- **Glittering generalities**: the opposite of name-calling, this technique associates a person or idea with a positive symbol.
- **Transfer**: a device by which the propagandist links the authority or prestige of something well-respected and revered, such as church or nation, to something he or she would have us accept.
- **Testimonial**: a technique in which a public figure or celebrity endorses a product, service or political candidate.
- **Plain folks**: an attempt to convince the audience that a prominent person and his or her ideas are *of the people*.
- **Bandwagon**: makes the appeal that *everyone else is doing it, and so should you*. In other words, *jump on the bandwagon*.
- **Fear**: a technique which plays on the fears of the audience; this is achieved by issuing a warning that disaster will occur if the audience does not follow a particular course of action.

These techniques are defined in further detail on the website *Propaganda Critic*, where you will also find examples of each technique. The site is included in the 'Resources for additional study' list at the end of this chapter.

■ Manifestos

KEY TERM

Manifesto – a written statement of the beliefs, aims and policies of an organization, especially a political party.

A manifesto is a written statement of the beliefs, aims and policies of an organization, especially a political party. Manifestos are usually issued by political parties before an election, with the purpose of persuading voters to support their platform. A manifesto is essentially an advertisement; the organization is selling its values and ideas. As such, manifestos incorporate many of the persuasive techniques listed above.

ACTIVITY 6: THE LANGUAGE OF MANIFESTOS

The following text is an abridged version of the *2017 General Election Manifesto* of the UK's Women's Equality Party. How does the text appeal to its audience? What persuasive techniques do you notice?

> WE have an eight point plan for a flourishing economy and an equal society that works better for everyone
>
> 1 **A caring economy**
>   WE offer a fresh approach that will build a sustainable caring economy that works for everyone.

2   Shared parental leave

WE will implement a fully equal system of nine months shared parental leave on 90% of pay, with a 3-month use-it-or-lose-it provision for each parent.

3   Free universal childcare

WE will implement full-time, high quality, free childcare for all children from the end of shared parental leave.

4   An end to violence against women

WE will repair the broken funding model for specialist services, including services that are for and led by BAME women. WE will put prevention, protection and provision at the heart of all our policies and WE will not rest until all women and girls are free from violence and harassment.

5   Unleashing women's talent

By reforming our education system and tackling the reductive and often hypersexualised depiction of women in the media, WE will unleash the talent of all.

6   Equality in health and social care

WE will make sure our healthcare system works for women and men alike, putting the furthest from equality first, and ensure that social care is recognised not as an adjunct to economic activity but as its underpinning.

7   Brexit

WE will build an immigration system with gender equality and social justice at its heart. WE will design trade deals that work for everybody. WE will make sure Brexit does not turn back the clock on gender equality through secondary legislation.

8   Invest in what matters

WE will invest in what matters and make sure our social infrastructure works as well as our physical infrastructure. WE will invest in homes, not houses, and restore our education, health care and social care systems. All our policies are costed and will not increase the burden on low and average income households.

Source: UK Women's Equality Party

■ Rhetorical devices

When we talk about the language of speeches and other types of argumentative writing, we are referring to **rhetoric**, defined by Oxford Dictionaries as: 'the art of effective or persuasive speaking or writing, especially the exploitation of figures of speech and other compositional techniques'. Those compositional techniques, or tools, that a speaker uses are called **rhetorical devices**.

Speech writers make use of many of the same devices that are found in poetry and prose, such as alliteration, allusion, hyperbole, personification and so on. In addition, there are certain rhetorical devices that are more typical of speeches. Definitions and examples of ten of the most common rhetorical devices are provided on the pages that follow, but this list should not be seen as exhaustive. You will note that many of these devices are figures of **repetition**, which is a key persuasive technique.

■ Anadiplosis

This is the repetition of the last word (or last terms) in one sentence, clause or phrase at, or very near, the beginning of the next sentence, clause or phrase.

Rhetoric – language designed to convince or persuade, making good use of compositional techniques.

Rhetorical devices – compositional techniques and tools that a speaker uses, for example, analogy.

Repetition – the repeated use of a word, phrase or image to draw attention to it.

■ Example: Margaret Thatcher's 'The Lady's Not For Turning' speech, 1980

'Of course our vision and our aims go far beyond the complex arguments of economics, but unless we get the economy right, we shall deny our people the opportunity to share that vision and to see beyond the narrow horizons of economic necessity. Without a healthy economy we can't have a <u>healthy society</u> and without a <u>healthy society</u> the economy won't stay healthy for long.'

Source: www.americanrhetoric.com

■ Analogy

Like similes and metaphors, an **analogy** is a comparison between two unlike things. However, unlike similes and metaphors, an analogy is presented as a way of furthering a line of reasoning or to support an argument.

■ Example: Henry Kissinger's memo to President Richard Nixon, 1969

'Withdrawal of US troops will become like salted peanuts to the American public; the more US troops come home, the more will be demanded.'

Source: https://history.state.gov/historicaldocuments/frus1969-76v01/d36

■ Anaphora

This is the repetition of a word or expression at the beginning of a number of sentences, clauses or phrases.

■ Example: Hillary Clinton's Democratic National Convention Address, 1996

'To raise a happy, healthy, and hopeful child, <u>it takes</u> a family; <u>it takes</u> teachers; <u>it takes</u> clergy; <u>it takes</u> business people; <u>it takes</u> community leaders; <u>it takes</u> those who protect our health and safety. <u>It takes</u> all of us.'

Source: www.americanrhetoric.com

■ Antimetabole

This is a figure of emphasis in which the words in one phrase or clause are replicated, exactly or closely, in reverse grammatical order in the next phrase or clause; an inverted order of repeated words in adjacent phrases or clauses (A-B, B-A).

■ Example: Ronald Reagan's speech 'Remarks at the Brandenburg Gate', 1987

'But we must remember a crucial fact: East and West do not <u>mistrust each other because we're armed</u>; <u>we're armed because we mistrust each other</u>.'

Source: www.americanrhetoric.com

■ Antithesis

This is the combination of two opposing ideas in a sentence, to achieve a contrasting effect.

■ Example: Martin Luther King, Jr's 'I Have a Dream' speech, 1963

> 'I have a dream that my four little children will one day live in a nation where they will <u>not be judged by the color of their skin</u> but <u>by the content of their character</u>. I have a *dream* today!'
>
> Source: www.americanrhetoric.com

■ Asyndeton

The omission of conjunctions (eg, *and*, *but*, *or*) in successive phrases or clauses.

■ Example: Richard Nixon's First Presidential Inaugural Address, 1969

> 'When we listen to the better angels of our nature, we find that they celebrate the <u>simple things, the basic things</u> – such as <u>goodness</u>, <u>decency</u>, <u>love</u>, <u>kindness</u>.'
>
> Source: www.americanrhetoric.com

■ Hypophora

A figure of speech in which a speaker raises a question and then immediately provides an answer. This is unlike a rhetorical question, which implies an answer.

■ Example: Bill Clinton's Democratic National Congress Acceptance Address, 1992

> 'What is George Bush doing about our economic problems<u>?</u> He has raised taxes on the people driving pickup trucks and lowered taxes on the people riding in limousines.'
>
> Source: www.americanrhetoric.com

■ Parallelism

This is the use of grammatically similar elements in sentences, or similarities in sound, meaning or rhythm.

■ Example: Abraham Lincoln's 'Gettysburg Address', 1863

> 'This nation, under God, shall have a new birth of freedom; and that government <u>of the people, by the people, for the people</u>, shall not perish from the earth.'
>
> Source: www.americanrhetoric.com

■ Polysyndeton

Polysyndeton is the opposite of asyndeton. It is the repetition of conjunctions (eg, *and*, *but*, *or*) in quick succession, without the use of commas to separate the ideas.

■ Example: Tom Brokaw's Second World War Memorial Dedication Address, 2004

'[Second World War] veterans here today will tell you that the first thing they noticed about basic training was breakfast. You could eat all that you wanted. Many got their first new pair of boots or trousers in basic training after a young life of hand-me-downs. Many will also tell you that before war came to America at Pearl Harbor they were opposed to this country getting involved. But when the Japanese attacked and the Germans declared war they converted overnight and transformed America into a mighty military machine – in uniform and factories and laboratories and shipyards and coal mines and farm fields and shops and offices.'

Source: www.americanrhetoric.com

■ Rhetorical question

A rhetorical question is a question that implies an answer or does not require an answer.

■ Non-verbal communication

Finally, it is important to note that if you are examining someone's delivery of a speech, rather than just the printed text, then you should also consider non-verbal communication such as eye contact and engagement with the audience, facial expressions and hand gestures.

ACTIVITY 7: RHETORICAL AND FIGURATIVE DEVICES

One of the most prominent orators of the 21st century is former US President Barack Obama. Parts of his first election victory speech are included below; you can read or view the whole speech online. Consider the purpose of Obama's speech. What rhetorical devices does he use and to what effect? Can you identify the types of appeals that he makes?

Barack Obama's Election Night Victory Speech

Grant Park, Illinois

November 4, 2008

If there is anyone out there who still doubts that America is a place where all things are possible; who still wonders if the dream of our founders is alive in our time; who still questions the power of our democracy, tonight is your answer.

It's the answer told by lines that stretched around schools and churches in numbers this
5 nation has never seen; by people who waited three hours and four hours, many for the very first time in their lives, because they believed that this time must be different; that their voice could be that difference.

It's the answer spoken by young and old, rich and poor, Democrat and Republican, black, white, Latino, Asian, Native American, gay, straight, disabled and not disabled – Americans
10 who sent a message to the world that we have never been a collection of Red States and Blue States: we are, and always will be, the United States of America.

It's the answer that led those who have been told for so long by so many to be cynical, and fearful, and doubtful of what we can achieve to put their hands on the arc of history and bend it once more toward the hope of a better day.

15 It's been a long time coming, but tonight, because of what we did on this day, in this election, at this defining moment, change has come to America.

Structure

Structure refers to the way in which a text is organized. Structure is not the same thing as layout, although layout is an element of structure. When you are analysing the structure of a text, it is important not to simply provide a description of the way the text looks (eg, 'This text is structured like a traditional essay because it is divided into paragraphs.' This is a very weak statement which says nothing about the function of a particular structural feature.). Instead, consider how the ideas are presented. A novel, for example, will follow a basic **plot** structure (exposition, rising action, climax, falling action, resolution). With a non-literary text, this may be trickier to recognize or identify, and the structure will vary from text to text. Ideas may be presented chronologically (eg, like in a biography), or they may be presented in a problem–solution format (eg, like in an advertisement). Other types of text structures include cause and effect, compare and contrast, sequence, classification–division, and description.

■ Conventions of text type

An important consideration when analysing non-literary texts is the conventions of the text type. Each text type has certain defining characteristics which distinguish it from other text types. You will not be expected to identify all of the characteristics of every possible text type, but you will have to demonstrate an understanding of how certain textual features help shape meaning. For example, if you can identify the kind of text you are dealing with through the recognition of certain features, this might help reveal something about the text's audience and purpose. It is also important to consider whether or not the text has deviated from its standard conventions and, if so, for what purpose.

■ Example: Reading between the lines of an interview

The text below is an interview from an online magazine called *The Missing Slate*. An interview is traditionally conducted to reveal information about the interviewee. In fact, in most written interviews, the personality of the interviewer will be absent, providing an almost disembodied voice. However, in this example we gain some insight into the interviewer as well.

themissingslate.com/2014/01/18/author-of-the-month-minoli-salgado/

Author of the month: Minoli Salgado

Minoli Salgado, The Missing Slate's Author of the Month for December, talks to assistant fiction editor Isra Ansari about voicing Sri Lanka's 'silenced' stories, the rise of 'South Asian' literature, and how writing felt like the only way to respond to the horrors of Sri Lanka's civil war.

In both 'The Breach' and your novel, 'A Little Dust on the Eyes', not only do you write specifically about Sri Lankan culture, your characters are predominantly female. You have also said that one of your abiding concerns is to give voice to some of the 'silenced' stories from Sri Lanka. Why do you use women to voice these unheard narratives?

I don't consciously choose to use women characters to articulate the silences I write about. In my novel and stories such as 'Releasing Marius' and 'The Map', men are also silent or silenced in various ways. But your question makes me aware that the silence of women might well be different from the silence of men. There are social expectations that reinforce the notion that women should not speak out at times when men might. Perhaps being raised, at least in part, in South Asia, I am very conscious of this. In this sense, silence is gendered and women and girls have more to overcome.

themissingslate.com/2014/01/18/author-of-the-month-minoli-salgado/

I am interested in this experience where speaking out is not simply a dangerous act, but a self-reclamation of sorts.

Sumana, your protagonist in 'The Breach', and her mother prepare to flee the bomb ridden area; the passage is intense and in its brevity captures desperation, fear and the will to survive. Where do you gather the inspiration to write about war and loss so captivatingly, portraying it vividly as if you were there yourself?

I wrote 'The Breach' in 2009, in the final stages of the civil war. This was a time when thousands of civilians were trapped in the tragically misnamed No Fire Zone. Like many diasporic* Sri Lankans, I followed the media coverage at the time. The news coverage abroad, here in the UK, was very different from that in the country. It was graphic, disturbing and very painful to watch. What was obvious to me at the time was that this was a human story, a tragedy that need not play out the way it did. I wrote this story then – writing was the only way I felt I could respond at the time. It was a way of wresting the human story from the competing versions of reality emerging from the war.

How significant are the influences of environment and history on your characters and their development in your stories?

That sounds a bit like an essay title! I think it's probably best answered by readers. Time and place are crucial factors for all writers of course.

Do you believe that the publishing world is, in any way, biased in favour of 'Western' authors? Does South Asian literature get the recognition it deserves?

The publishing world is a very big place and it's expanding as we speak. Globalization and the digital age have changed things a lot. Though recognition may still be played out through metropolitan circuits, things have opened up.

When I began writing, South Asian writers in English, both diasporic and national, were beginning to make their mark in Western universities. They were initially labeled as such but things have changed as many of them […] have transformed the literary landscape. Writers can now be recognized as international writers who happen to come from South Asia. And this wealth of talent continues to grow. I think the difficulty is not so much in getting South Asian literature recognized, but finding a space for it in the market that doesn't compromise its literary integrity by putting exclusive value on its cultural status as 'South Asian'.

We could talk at length about writing techniques, the role of women in South Asian literature, numerous other topics … but I'm sure our readers would be interested to know which authors have inspired you and been there throughout your growth as a writer and person. Who would be on your essential reading list?

Ah, reading lists. I must admit I have a lot of those. There are writers I read for pleasure, writers I read to learn from, writers I read because they teach us about how literature has evolved and developed in ways that have brought us to where we are, writers I read because they have been recommended to me by friends. When I was a teenager I was addicted to nineteenth-century realist novels, then, at university, I lost and found myself in contemporary writing and postcolonial literature. So it is difficult to put together an essential reading list, as it were, because I read very widely and for different reasons. Having said that, I do have an abiding preference for beautifully written, historical novels with an epic reach, and for lyrical poetry that carries me into other worlds and selves.

Minoli Salgado's novel 'A Little Dust on the Eyes' *is to be published later this year.*

*Diasporic: relating to the the dispersion or spread of any people from their original homeland

The text reads more like a conversation in which both participants are equally engaged. We learn that the interviewer has read at least two of the writer's works, is curious about the role of women in those works, asks multi-level questions that seem to have a more cultural than literary agenda, seems to be working from a prepared list of questions, and so on. The text could have been presented in the form of an article or profile piece, but the decision to include the interview transcript and break from the more traditional conventions of an interview is perhaps intended to reflect the wider purpose of the magazine, which is highlighted in a blurb at the top of the article online: 'The Missing Slate is a "borderless" magazine with a culturally and intellectually diverse team that believes if art can't be quantified, it can't be mapped either.'

■ Opinion column

An opinion column is, as the name would suggest, an opinionated piece of writing, the aim of which is to persuade – and perhaps, to a certain extent, to entertain. Opinion columns feature in most major newspapers and are usually the work of permanent staff writers who have gained a reputation for their style and treatment of current events.

An opinion column is similar to an editorial and an op-ed (which stands for *opposite the editorial*), but the key difference is in authorship. An editorial is written by the editor of a newspaper or magazine, often outlining their stance on a particular issue or justifying choices they have made within the current publication. An op-ed is most often written by someone outside of the publication in response to an issue of universal appeal.

ACTIVITY 8: TEXTUAL FEATURES OF AN OPINION COLUMN

Read the following opinion column from *The Harvard Crimson* website and identify the key features that you notice. What elements would you say characterize this text type?

www.thecrimson.com/column/socially-liberal-fiscally-liberal/article/2018/2/6/brooks-ending-social-media/

The Case for Ending Social Media

By Henry N. Brooks, Contributing Opinion Writer

February 6, 2018

It's high time we admitted that Facebook and Twitter are pernicious technologies. Those who doubt this haven't taken stock of the last two years.

In Jan. 2018, an online firestorm broke out after social media users circulated a sound bite from Psychology professor Steven A. Pinker, in which he referred to the 'highly literate, highly intelligent' alt-right. Though Pinker hardly intended flattery, he drew fire from the left as the 'darling' of racists, while the far-right quickly made him out as a liberal, Jewish Uncle Tom.

Last August, Professor Kyle P. Quinn at the University of Arkansas and his wife began to fear for their safety when Twitter users, believing him to be one of the neo-Nazi marchers at Charlottesville, instigated a barrage of hate mail that included violent threats. When someone publicly tweeted his home address, Quinn and his wife had to go into hiding until the crusade against them subsided.

In Nov. 2016, the presidential election went to then-Republican nominee Donald Trump, though suspicions of Russian hacking mired the results. Since the election, news sources have reported the possibility that the Russian government activated several thousand fake social media profiles (like it was accused of doing in France) in order to influence the election through propaganda.

Commentators have yet to aggregate these and other incidents in a way that suggests a pattern. Although criticism of social media has waxed in recent years—as society has entered a stage of advanced interconnectivity—

most of it has stayed the neoliberal course. The result has been a body of essays calling on individuals to police their own indulgent behaviors and framing overuse in pathological terms (so-called 'Facebook Addiction Disorder,' for example). When confronted with quagmires like Pinker's, the usual critics ignore the manifest disjunction between individual attitudes (which are often polite) and collective behaviors (which can contradict individuals' behavioral tendencies). They also forfeit the possibility that social technologies stand to profit from our collective degeneracy. By locating the problem in our own weakness of will, these critics offer very little in the way of actual critical analysis.

Recently, some high-ranking members of the social media apparat have broken with the party line to express concern. Last winter, former Facebook vice president for user growth Chamath Palihapitiya announced that Facebook was providing the 'tools that are ripping apart the social fabric.' Since then, early Facebook investor Roger McNamee published three articles deriding the company for its intended addictive quality and hands-off approach to fake news. McNamee even called on Facebook's CEO, Mark E. Zuckerberg, to report before Congress for his company's negligence.

McNamee and Palihapitiya are welcome to wage their crusades, but their calls for reform are ultimately toothless. Palihapitiya told listeners that when he left Facebook, he forbade his own children from creating accounts. That was all he could do. McNamee proposed a government investigation into Facebook's reckless attitude toward misinformation, but he himself has since acknowledged the insufficiency of federal oversight.

This author offers an alternative to the usual incrementalism. Zuckerberg and his cohort should surrender their platforms.

www.thecrimson.com/column/socially-liberal-fiscally-liberal/article/2018/2/6/brooks-ending-social-media/

In the present age of advanced technology, our laissez-faire attitude toward the digital lifeworld has left us with competing assessments of our technological circumstances. One view asserts that technology—like Kant's 'wit, judgment, and … talents'—is good or bad depending on its use. So it goes that if television broadcasts propaganda it is bad, and if it broadcasts Sesame Street, it is good. The second view, which differs only slightly, holds that technology can be neither good nor bad, as it is merely a medium. The episodes in Cambridge, Arkansas, and America at-large suggest that both of these views are lacking.

Marshall McLuhan, the Canadian media theorist, famously resolved this question with the formulation that 'the medium is the message.' McLuhan meant that the vehicles through which content is transmitted have their own social effects, independent of what exactly they carry.

Television, according to this view, didn't affect American households just by its sitcoms and dramas. The television itself inaugurated an era in which people read less because they could watch. It destroyed the sanctity of the dinner table by drawing the family to its evening programming. Thus, whether the monitor picked up the Muppets or Les Crane, social life was changed irrevocably.

Television has benefits, of course. A 'bad' medium can still transmit 'good' content or demonstrate 'good' use. This has been a common talking point among social justice activists, who acknowledge that social media has made educating and mobilizing easier than ever. Yet a bad medium still corrupts. The rise of 'slacktivism' has only become possible with platforms like Facebook and Twitter, which function entirely through optics, making it easy to look the part of an activist. We can't take this to mean progress.

Until now, the extent of our criticism of social media has been to rearticulate the 'pull yourself up by your bootstraps' philosophy: cut down on Facebook time, monitor children's Twitter and Instagram access, only follow reputable pages. But the time for these individualistic efforts is long past when professors must flee their homes to avoid a mob.

The medium itself is rotten, facilitating a style of insurgent politics that exacerbates disagreement, scales misinformation, and robs users of focus. If Zuckerberg still reads The Crimson, he should take this as a friendly call to action: for the good of the culture, shut your platform down.

Creative extension: You be the columnist

Now that you have familiarized yourself with the characteristics of an opinion column (comparing this with the notes at the end of the book), it's your turn to be the columnist. Choose a timely issue or current event that you feel passionate about and write an argumentative piece in the style of a columnist whose work you admire.

Conclusion

We have examined a variety of non-literary texts in this chapter through the lenses of specific language and literary devices. *Language* is a broad term encompassing many different elements, but focusing on the elements we have outlined in this chapter should provide you with a good foundation on which to build your individual interpretation and appreciation of texts.

Resources for additional study

- Carter, R, Bowring, M, Goddard, A and Reah, D (2007), *Working with Texts: A Core Introduction to Language Analysis* (Intertext), London: Routledge. This is the core text in the Intertext series and provides a good overview of a range of texts. This series includes other useful texts such as *The Language of Newspapers* by Danuta Reah and *The Language of Advertising* by Angela Goddard.

- The *American Rhetoric* website (**www.americanrhetoric.com/**) is a comprehensive source on the art of rhetoric. It includes definitions and examples of key rhetorical devices (along with many more obscure devices), as well as a bank of speeches organized by category (eg, Top 100 Speeches, Great New Speeches, Obama Speeches).

- Propaganda Critic (**https://propagandacritic.com/**) is a website which promotes propaganda analysis. It is a comprehensive source of information and features articles on social media and fake news as well as examples of propaganda from various forms of media.

Works cited

'American Rhetoric: The Power Of Oratory In The United States', Web, accessed 3 December 2018, *Americanrhetoric.com*, 2019, Web, accessed 4 December 2018, **https://www.americanrhetoric.com/**

Ansari, I., 'Minoli Salgado interview', *The Missing Slate*, 18 January 2014, Web, accessed 3 December 2018, **https://themissingslate.com/2014/01/18/author-of-the-month-minoli-salgado/**

Brooks, Henry N., 'The Case for Ending Social Media', *The Harvard Crimson*, 6 February 2018, Web, accessed 19 November 2018, **www.thecrimson.com/column/socially-liberal-fiscally-liberal/article/2018/2/6/brooks-ending-social-media/**

'Caravan of Migrants Swells to 7000 As They Eye US', *Mail Online*, 21 October 2018, Web, accessed 19 November 2018, **www.dailymail.co.uk/news/article-6300649/Caravan-migrants-swells-5-000-eye-US.html**

Crandell, Bradshaw, V&A Collections, 'Are You A Girl With A Star-Spangled Heart?' poster (1943), Web, accessed 3 December 2018, **http://collections.vam.ac.uk/item/O101036/are-you-a-girl-with-poster-crandell-bradshaw/**

Delwiche, Aaron, 'Propaganda Is Everywhere – Propaganda Critic', *Propaganda Critic*, 18 October 2018, Web, accessed 4 December 2018, **https://propagandacritic.com/index.php/core-concepts/propaganda-is-everywhere/**

'Desperate Central American Refugees Cross Into Mexico From River', *The Guardian*, 21 October 2018, Web, accessed 19 November 2018, **www.theguardian.com/world/2018/oct/21/honduran-migrant-caravan-crosses-into-mexico-through-river**

Dolasia, Meera, 'Oxford Dictionaries 'Word Of The Year' Is … An Emoji?', DOGONews, 17 November 2015, Web, accessed 28 January 2019, **www.dogonews.com/2015/11/17/oxford-dictionaries-word-of-the-year-is-an-emoji**

Gardiner, Meg, 'It's alive', Lying for a Living blog, 27 July 2018, Web, accessed 3 December 2018, **https://meggardiner.wordpress.com/2006/07/27/hello-world/**

Gilbert, Elizabeth, *Eat Pray Love*, London: Bloomsbury Publishing, 2006 (print).

Gonzalez, Emma, 'Emma Gonzalez's powerful March For Our Lives speech in full', *YouTube* (recorded and uploaded 24 Mar 2018), Web, accessed 3 December 2018, **www.youtube.com/watch?v=u46HzTGVQhg**

Kissinger, Henry, 'Memo to Richard Nixon', 10 September 1969, Office of the Historian, Web, accessed 3 December 2018, **https://history.state.gov/historicaldocuments/frus1969-76v01/d36**

'Swamp water', Yahoo Groups post 'Microscopy as a hobby or profession', 24 October 2004, Web, accessed 29 January 2019, **https://groups.yahoo.com/neo/groups/Microscope/conversations/messages/20587**

Obama, Barack, 'President-Elect Victory Speech', 4 November 2008, American Rhetoric, Web, accessed 28 January 2019, **www.americanrhetoric.com/speeches/convention2008/barackobamavictoryspeech.htm**

Owen, Wilfred, 'Letter To Susan Owen' (France, 31 Oct 1918) [online facsimile], The Harry Ransom Center/The Wilfred Owen Literary Estate via *First World War Poetry Digital Archive*, Web, accessed 3 December 2018, **http://ww1lit.nsms.ox.ac.uk/ww1lit/collections/document/5262**

Oxfam GB, Yemen Crisis Appeal (2018), Web, accessed 3 December 2018, **www.oxfam.org.uk/what-we-do/emergency-response/yemen-crisis**

Rhetorical Figures in Sound, *American Rhetoric*, Web, accessed 3 December 2018, **www.americanrhetoric.com/rhetoricaldevicesinsound.htm**

White, Michael and Cole, Peter, 'How To Write Columns', *The Guardian*, 25 September 2018, Web, accessed 19 November 2018, **www.theguardian.com/books/2008/sep/25/writing.journalism.columns**

Women's Equality Party, *2017 General Election Manifesto*, Web, accessed 3 December 2018, (2017), **www.womensequality.org.uk/manifesto**

Woolf, Virginia, 'The Art of Biography' in *The Death of The Moth, and other essays*, The University of Adelaide, 2015, Ebooks.Adelaide.Edu.Au, Web, accessed 3 December 2018, **https://ebooks.adelaide.edu.au/w/woolf/virginia/w91d/chapter23.html**

3 Approaches to literary works

As part of your DP English programme, you will be required to read a minimum of four (SL) or six (HL) literary works. Those works will come from the following four forms: poetry, drama, prose fiction and literary non-fiction. At the standard level, students must study works from two of those four forms, while at the higher level, they must study three types. The study of literary works is in addition to the study of non-literary texts (such as those you were introduced to in Chapter 2) but comprising equal time. Your approach to analysing those works will, in many ways, be similar to your approach to non-literary texts. However, there are some features of a literary work which you will not encounter in other genres, such as blogs or news accounts, that you will encounter in the course.

This chapter will take you through three particular features of literary works, and includes examples from poetry, prose fiction and drama in each section. We cannot cover all the important approaches to literary works in this one relatively short chapter, so the objective is to help you master the use of several key tools: interpreting the role of the narrator, figurative language and structure. A list of suggested reading at the end of the chapter will point you to some additional tools that you may wish to consult in order to develop your interpretive skills to a more sophisticated degree.

What is a literary work as opposed to a non-literary text?

KEY TERM

Analysis – the reader's observation of how the narrator is telling the story, the identification of the various elements of that story-telling process, and the explanation of how those elements create meaning.

What we usually mean when we talk about a *literary* work is that it has intentionally been created as a work of art. That usually means that the work is fiction; that is, it does not recount events that happened in real life. Just because a work is fiction, however, does not mean that it contains no truth. The truth you will encounter in any artwork is a truth about the artist's vision of human experience and of the world around us. The *facts* and events in a work of literature are not literally true; however, they reveal broader truths about the way in which we experience our lives. Given the nature of this course, you are more likely to study poetry, prose fiction and drama than literary non-fiction, just because you will be reading a good deal of non-literary non-fiction. Your teacher may choose, however, to include one or more works of literary non-fiction. If so, you would treat the **analysis** of those works just as you would treat the analysis of literary fiction.

> The relationship between poetry and fiction is somewhat complicated. Lyric poetry, especially, is not necessarily fiction in the same way that novels and short stories are. However, poetry is still art, not autobiography, opinion writing, travel writing or any other form of non-fiction. Sylvia Plath, who is commonly considered to be one of the world's most confessional poets, objected strongly to the idea that any poetry – hers included – is simply autobiography. She emphasised the fact that poetry is art (Uroff 105). The point is that poets are artists; they may work with ideas and events very similar to what they have experienced themselves in their personal lives, but to create a poem they transform that experience. Sophisticated readers keep that distinction very much in mind.

■ Relationship between reader and writer

In a literary work, as opposed to a non-literary text, the author is not making an overt attempt to influence the reader directly. As you saw in Chapter 2, the voice in most of the types of non-literary texts you will study is essentially (though not completely or perfectly) the voice of the author. The author speaks, as it were, directly to you, the reader, in an effort to affect your ideas, values and/or beliefs. If the author could speak to you directly, in person, presumably he or she would speak to you much the same way as he or she does through the text. The interaction between author and reader can be conceived as follows:

Real author →→ Text ←— Real reader

There are, of course, certain issues that arise when the reader and writer communicate through a text; hence the strategies detailed in Chapter 2. However, the transaction involved in a non-literary text is as direct a communication as is possible to have through a text.

KEY TERM

Fabula – a fictional world created by the writer.

The interaction between author and reader in a literary work, however, cannot be assumed to be so direct. With literary works, the writer creates a narrator who tells a story about, or in some other way introduces the reader to, an imagined situation. That situation might be based on events that actually happened or include things which exist in the real world, but regardless, the author constructs a **fabula**, a fictional world, and chooses what people and actions will occur in it. The reader's job is to interpret the text. That involves figuring out the nature of the narrator, whether he or she can be trusted, and then working out the implications of those characters and events. The reader does not have direct access to the writer, and the writer does not have direct access to the reader. The text does not state directly what the author thinks or feels. The reader has to observe the actions and attitudes of the narrator and characters, then make judgements about whether those actions and attitudes are positive or negative and what they reveal about the way people live and react in the real world. You can imagine the transaction this way:

Real author →→ Implied author →→ Narrator →→ Text ←— Implied reader ←— Real reader

Literary works are not, therefore, fundamentally persuasive. If a reader's outlook, feelings or beliefs are changed by reading a literary work, that is the result of indirect influence. Change arises from the reader's thinking over the interpretation of the text and finding him or herself in agreement with the fundamental principles which underlie it.

One important point to keep in mind about a literary work, then, is that the author does not have to consider the audience in the same way that the author of a non-literary text does. The audience for the literary work is whoever can read and understand that text. Naturally, the author does consider audience in some very basic ways: there is a big difference, for example, between a work written for young children and one written for adults, but the author does not have to take into consideration what an audience will like or dislike or respond to in a particular way. The author of the literary work is not trying to manipulate the thinking of the reader; the author of the literary work is creating a piece of art that will be released into the world, which will then find its audience and have an effect on the world which the author could not necessarily predict or control.

Most literary works are fictional, which is integral to the indirect nature of the communication between the author and the reader. Some non-fiction texts, however, can be seen as literary works. These are usually essays – often memoirs – such as essays by Alice Walker or Jorge Luis Borges. These literary essays will overlap with the category of non-literary texts in your English programme. You will be directed by your teacher as to whether you are to treat the non-fiction in your course as literary or non-literary works for the purpose of the curriculum. The most common situation will likely be that all of your non-fiction works will come under the heading of non-literary texts, but definitely listen to what your teacher tells you about how to handle those works.

Works in translation

A significant number of the works you study for your English Language and Literature course will be read in translation. Translators must struggle with many difficulties in trying to create an effective translation. Just one example is the problem of what to do with texts that are written in a particular metrical form requiring a specific number of syllables per line. For instance, Shakespeare's work is predominantly written in lines of ten syllables. When translating his work into Russian, the translator has to decide whether to extend the lines or whether to cut the number of lines by half, because the average Russian word has just about twice as many syllables as the average English word. *Hamlet* runs for more than four hours if performed in its entirety; if a Russian translator decides to keep all of the content Shakespeare wrote, his version would be nearly twice as long.

In an essay entitled 'Lost in Translation', novelist Tom Robbins demonstrates just how dramatically different a translation can be from an original. This is the first paragraph from the prologue to his novel *Jitterbug Perfume:*

> The beet is the most intense of vegetables. The radish, admittedly, is more feverish, but the fire of the radish is a cold fire, the fire of discontent not of passion. Tomatoes are lusty enough, yet there runs through tomatoes an undercurrent of frivolity. Beets are deadly serious. (209)

Then he offers an English translation of the same novel in Czech. This, in other words, is what Czech readers would get from their version of the novel:

> Among all vegetables, the red beet is the most passionate. The radish may be hotter, but her heat soars in the cold flame of anxiety, not passion. Tomatoes may be sufficiently energetic, but then, they are known for their carelessness. The beet is mortally serious. (210)

You can see from the differences in vocabulary just from this very short section that the choices that translators make have significant implications. The idea of the feverish radish which burns with a cold fire is quite different from the idea of a radish which is anxious.

Whenever you are interpreting a work that you are studying in translation, therefore, understand that you are studying the work of the interpreter, not the work of the author. Unless you are fluent in the language of the original, and have access to the text in that language, you will likely not be able to make a comparison between the two versions, so you will have no choice but to work solely in the translation. In that case, then, you just need to be aware that you are not getting the author's original intent.

Interpreting literary works

You need to understand the indirect nature of the reader–writer relationship in order to be able to interpret literary works effectively. In this chapter we will look at the role of the narrator, figurative language (particularly the nature of **symbols** and **metaphors**) and structure in order to help you do this.

KEY TERMS

Symbol – a comparison between something the author wants the reader to think about and another element, often discussed as a subset of the category of metaphor.

Metaphor – a comparison between two things.

KEY TERMS

Reliable narrator – a trustworthy narrator who accurately presents what the author thinks, believes, feels or values.

Unreliable narrator – an untrustworthy narrator who does not speak in accordance with the author's intentions.

Implied author – the author that the text implies, constructed through reading.

■ The role of the narrator

In a literary work, either prose or poetry, the role of the narrator is crucial. Because the narrator is a creation, often a character in the work, the first question the reader must pose is the question of whether or not the narrator is reliable: can we trust the narrator to be an accurate representation of what the author thinks, believes, feels, or values? If we have a **reliable narrator**, then we have a fairly direct line to the author's thinking.

The concept of the **unreliable narrator**, on the other hand, was developed by Wayne Booth in the 1960s. In his *Rhetoric of Fiction*, Booth describes the reliable narrator thus: 'For lack of better terms, I have called a narrator *reliable* when he speaks for or acts in accordance with the norms of the work (which is to say, the implied author's norms), *unreliable* when he does not' (159).

The **implied author** is the author that the text implies. The term acknowledges that we do not have direct access to the author's thinking, constrained as we are by our need to work through the narrator, so we cannot say for certain that we know the *real* author. We can only construct, through our reading, an implied author.

Booth goes on to explain that an unreliable narrator is unconsciously unreliable (159). He or she is not deliberately lying because a lying narrator knows the truth. An unreliable narrator believes that he or she is telling the truth, but is wrong, either because he or she lacks intelligence or observation skills, is deluded by personal desires or biases, or has some other mental or emotional failing which keeps him or her from seeing reality as it is.

An unreliable narrator is, well, unreliable! You cannot believe what an unreliable narrator tells you – at least in part. You can probably believe most of the facts that the narrator reports, but you cannot believe his or her interpretation of those facts. An unreliable narrator does still help us understand what the author is trying to convey, we just have to understand that the unreliable narrator shows us something that the author does not believe is right or true. The author asks us to look at an unreliable narrator and judge the narrator's failings.

A famous example of an unreliable narrator is the speaker of Robert Browning's poem 'My Last Duchess'.

■ Example: 'My Last Duchess' by Robert Browning

<blockquote>

She had
A heart—how shall I say?—too soon made glad,
Too easily impressed; she liked whate'er
She looked on, and her looks went everywhere.
5 Sir, 'twas all one! My favour at her breast,
The dropping of the daylight in the West,
The bough of cherries some officious fool
Broke in the orchard for her, the white mule
She rode with round the terrace—all and each
10 Would draw from her alike the approving speech,
Or blush, at least. She thanked men—good! but thanked
Somehow—I know not how—as if she ranked
My gift of a nine-hundred-years-old name
With anybody's gift. Who'd stoop to blame
15 This sort of trifling? Even had you skill

</blockquote>

> In speech—which I have not—to make your will
> Quite clear to such an one, and say, 'Just this
> Or that in you disgusts me; here you miss,
> Or there exceed the mark' —and if she let
> 20 Herself be lessoned so, nor plainly set
> Her wits to yours, forsooth, and made excuse—
> E'en then would be some stooping; and I choose
> Never to stoop. Oh, sir, she smiled, no doubt,
> Whene'er I passed her; but who passed without
> 25 Much the same smile? This grew; I gave commands;
> Then all smiles stopped together. There she stands
> As if alive.

The speaker is describing a portrait of his 'last', that is *former*, because she is now dead, wife. At first glance, we might think that his account of her behaviour is balanced and logical – certainly his tone is calm and seems objective. But if we read more carefully, we start to see signs that the speaker is narcissistic and incapable of making proper judgements because he is eaten up with jealousy. At line 5, for example, we see a sign of anger in that explanation point. The speaker is amazed that his wife could have been equally impressed by his favour as by the sun setting. At line 13, we see that he has excessive pride in his 'nine-hundred-years-old name' and that it should be rated much higher than the gift of any other nobody (line 14). In lines 15–23, the speaker reveals that even if he thought he could teach his wife to show him proper respect – that is, much more respect than anyone or anything else deserved – he would not do it, because to have to do so would require him to 'stoop'. His pride is extreme. He expected his wife to adore and respect him above all other people and experiences – and he expected her to do so without having to be told that that is what he expected. Finally, in lines 23–6, we realize that when his wife dared to smile in the same way at others as she smiled at him, he had her killed.

This poem relies on a classic unreliable narrator. This speaker believes that he understood his wife perfectly. He blames her entirely for her behaviour, which he saw as not merely inappropriate, but actually an offence worthy of death. Careful readers will understand that the author does not agree with the narrator. We see that the narrator had a charming and friendly young woman for a wife. She was apparently appreciative of all things, including sunsets and cherry blossoms and animals. She was, in short, a nice person. Browning is expecting us to look at the speaker and to judge the Duke harshly for his horrific behaviour.

ACTIVITY 1: 'THE TELL-TALE HEART' BY EDGAR ALLAN POE

Read the short extract from Poe's short story. What indicators are there in this paragraph, the first of the story, that the narrator is not reliable? Note them down and then write a short description of what you think the author wishes his readers to think of this narrator. Then read the notes at the end of the book.

> True! – nervous – very, very dreadfully nervous I had been and am; but why will you say that I am mad? The disease had sharpened my senses – not destroyed – not dulled them. Above all was the sense of hearing acute. I heard all things in the heaven and in the earth. I heard many things in hell. How, then, am I mad? Hearken! and observe how healthily – how calmly
> 5 I can tell you the whole story.

■ The narrator and drama

One of the main differences between a drama and prose fiction is that most plays do not have narrators. If you do have a narrator in a drama, then your job as reader/viewer is to examine the reliability of that narrator just as you would in a prose text or a poem. *Our Town* by Thornton Wilder, for example, has a narrator who comes out on stage and calls up scenes for the audience to watch.

In plays without a narrator to interpret either as a reliable guide to the author's thinking or an indirect one through his or her unreliability, the reader or viewer has to understand the author's purpose through interpreting the significance of the characters and the events. Characters in a drama can speak or behave in ways that are misguided or delusional just as the narrator in a novel or a speaker of a poem can. The important point for you as a reader of literary works, or as an audience member at a performance of a play is that you cannot just assume that the author approves of all the characters in the work. Some of the greatest excitement in interpreting literature comes from studying the characters, including narrators or speakers, with an eye to finding out which ones are trustworthy and which ones are examples of failed persons.

In *Cyrano de Bergerac*, by Edmond Rostand, for example, we have in the main character, Cyrano, a person who is terribly insecure due to having been born with an extraordinarily big, ugly nose. To cover up that insecurity, he has developed a persona that is brave to the point of recklessness. In one scene, he takes on and beats one hundred men who have been sent to kill him. As a reader or viewer of the play, you can begin to pick up on Cyrano's problem early on, in this exchange between Cyrano and a Viscount who does not know Cyrano.

■ Example: *Cyrano de Bergerac* by Edmond Rostand

> DE GUICHE: Will no one put him down? …
>
> THE VISCOUNT: No one? But wait!
> I'll treat him to … one of my quips! … See here! …
> (He goes up to Cyrano, who is watching him, and with a conceited air):
> 5 Sir, your nose is … hmm … it is … very big!
>
> CYRANO (gravely): Very!
>
> THE VISCOUNT (laughing): Ha!
>
> CYRANO (imperturbably): Is that all? …
>
> THE VISCOUNT: What do you mean?
>
> 10 CYRANO: Ah no! young blade! That was a trifle short!
> You might have said at least a hundred things
> By varying the tone … like this, suppose, …
> Aggressive: 'Sir, if I had such a nose
> I'd amputate it!' Friendly: 'When you sup
> 15 It must annoy you, dipping in your cup;
> You need a drinking-bowl of special shape!'
> Descriptive: 'Tis a rock! … a peak! … a cape!
> – A cape, forsooth! 'Tis a peninsular!'
> Curious: 'How serves that oblong capsular?
> 20 For scissor-sheath? Or pot to hold your ink?'

Gracious: 'You love the little birds, I think?
I see you've managed with a fond research
To find their tiny claws a roomy perch!'
Truculent: 'When you smoke your pipe … suppose
25 That the tobacco-smoke spouts from your nose –
Do not the neighbors, as the fumes rise higher,
Cry terror-struck: 'The chimney is afire'?'
Considerate: 'Take care, … your head bowed low
By such a weight … lest head o'er heels you go!'
30 Tender: 'Pray get a small umbrella made,
Lest its bright color in the sun should fade!'
Pedantic: 'That beast Aristophanes
Names Hippocamelelephantoles
Must have possessed just such a solid lump
35 Of flesh and bone, beneath his forehead's bump!'
Cavalier: 'The last fashion, friend, that hook?
To hang your hat on? 'Tis a useful crook!'
Emphatic: 'No wind, O majestic nose,
Can give THEE cold! – save when the mistral blows!'
40 Dramatic: 'When it bleeds, what a Red Sea!'
Admiring: 'Sign for a perfumery!'
Lyric: 'Is this a conch? … a Triton you?'
Simple: 'When is the monument on view?'
Rustic: 'That thing a nose? Marry-come-up!
45 'Tis a dwarf pumpkin, or a prize turnip!'
Military: 'Point against cavalry!'
Practical: 'Put it in a lottery!
Assuredly 'twould be the biggest prize!'
Or … parodying Pyramus' sighs …
50 'Behold the nose that mars the harmony
Of its master's phiz! blushing its treachery!'
– Such, my dear sir, is what you might have said,
Had you of wit or letters the least jot:
But, O most lamentable man! – of wit
55 You never had an atom, and of letters
You have three letters only! – they spell Ass!
And – had you had the necessary wit,
To serve me all the pleasantries I quote
Before this noble audience … e'en so,
60 You would not have been let to utter one –
Nay, not the half or quarter of such jest!
I take them from myself all in good part,
But not from any other man that breathes!

KEY TERM

Monologue –
an (often long)
speech given by
one person or
character.

In that long **monologue**, Cyrano makes 18 different jokes about the size of his nose, which makes him seem charming and funny, as well as quick-witted and intelligent; however, so many jokes is overkill. The character protests too much that he doesn't care about the size of his nose. He also ends his monologue by pointing out that he, and only he, may make jokes about his nose. He will permit no other man to say anything derogatory. That kind of extreme defensiveness is always a sign of insecurity, so the audience learns early on to watch for Cyrano's sensitivity to his physical appearance. The playwright has signalled to us that this character, though appealing, is damaged and so may not be totally reliable. Your job in analysing the characters is the same as it would be for analysing the narrator, if there were one.

A final note about drama and the narrator: if you are reading a play, rather than watching it, you will have access to a narrator of sorts in the form of the stage directions. By reading the stage directions, you can get information that a viewer of the play cannot get. In an article for *American Literature*, Nancy Anne Cluck makes this observation about the stage directions in Tennessee Williams' play, *The Glass Menagerie*.

■ Example: 'Showing or Telling: Narrators in the Drama of Tennessee Williams' by Nancy Anne Cluck

> The philosopher becomes poet in some of his narration. For example, he tells us in I, vi, that 'It is about five on a Friday evening of late spring' which comes 'scattering poems in the sky' (II, vi, 69). There is no way that, through set or actions, the audience could know this spring scatters poems. At the beginning of this same scene,
> 5 the following description is given of Laura: 'A fragile, unearthly prettiness has come out in Laura: she is like a piece of translucent glass touched by light, given momentary radiance, not actual, not lasting' (88), American Literature (69). Once again the reader, not the theatre audience, has the advantage of the poetic metaphor. (Cluck 87–8)

KEY TERMS

Tenor – in relation
to a metaphor, the
tenor is the thing
or object that
the author wants
the reader to
understand better.

Vehicle – in
relation to a
metaphor, the
vehicle is the
thing or object
that the author is
comparing their
subject to.

Extended
metaphor – a
metaphor used
throughout a
poem or a lengthy
passage, often to
point out certain
characteristics of
the subject for the
reader to consider.

When you are reading a play, therefore, you will encounter something like a narrator, which you will not encounter in the live theatre, but you will always be able to assume that that 'narrator' is highly reliable.

Figurative language and other literary strategies

There are a great many literary strategies which, if you know how to spot and interpret them, will help you develop an understanding of the author's meaning. We will cover a few of the more common strategies here.

■ Metaphor

A metaphor is a comparison between two things. There are names for the two parts of a metaphor: **tenor**, which is the name for the thing in the text that the author wants the reader to understand better, and **vehicle**, which is the name for the thing to which that element is being compared. In his song, *A Red, Red Rose*, Robert Burns famously wrote:

O my Luve is like a red, red rose
That's newly sprung in June;

Love (luve) is the tenor and the rose is the vehicle. In this case, of course, the line is a simile, a type of metaphor which makes the comparison overt through the use of *like* or *as*.

Your job is to consider the nature of the vehicle and to decide which features of the vehicle can be seen to shed light on the tenor. In the case of the metaphor of the rose for love, you have to think about what a rose is like, and why a rose might help us understand love better. Here are some characteristics of roses:

- There are many hundreds – even thousands – of varieties.

- Roses are very beautiful.

- Roses are more beautiful when they are young and fresh, and as they age they tend to become overblown, and then they start losing petals and eventually they die.

- Despite their beauty, roses have thorns, and if you are not careful about how you handle them, you can hurt yourself.

- Roses smell sweet (they appeal to more than one sense).

We could keep on brainstorming ideas. Often, in fact, the ideas that you think of after you have listed all the most obvious features turn out to be the best ones. We can already see, however, how roses make a good metaphor for love: all of the characteristics listed here can be seen to apply to love, and if we think about all those aspects of love, instead of just thinking about the excitement and joy that we feel in the first blush of new love, we understand love in a more complex way than we did before.

The idea of love being like a red rose might seem clichéd by now, but in 1794, when Burns wrote the song, it might have been a fresh metaphor. Better writers will, in fact, come up with new metaphors – new comparisons – to make you think about things in a way in which you have never considered them before.

In Carol Ann Duffy's poem 'Valentine', for instance, she uses an **extended metaphor** of an onion to stand for love. An extended metaphor is one that is used throughout a poem or a lengthy passage. Typically, authors use extended metaphors to point to numerous characteristics of the vehicle that they want us to think about. In this case, the onion is an unusual metaphor, as we are not accustomed to thinking of love as being like an onion. Onions smell bad and they make us cry. But as Duffy points out, they also have many layers, and the inside of the onion is initially obscured by a brown paper-like coating. Onions flavour our food. They grow in rings, like wedding rings, and so on. Thinking further, love can be seen to have similar characteristics, such as hidden secrets which sometimes cause pain and sorrow. If you read the poem, you will see that the poet has pointed out many features of an onion which help us see love in a totally new light.

KEY TERM	ACTIVITY 2: SHAKESPEARE'S SONNET 73

KEY TERM

Quatrain – a stanza of four lines.

ACTIVITY 2: SHAKESPEARE'S SONNET 73

Read the following sonnet by William Shakespeare. Each **quatrain** contains a different metaphor that Shakespeare uses to help the audience understand the nature of ageing. The first quatrain compares growing old to a winter tree, the second quatrain compares growing old to the end of a day and the third quatrain compares growing old to a dying fire.

In each case, note the particular features of the metaphor that Shakespeare points out, and then explain what each feature reveals about the process of growing old. When you have finished, you can read the activity notes at the end of the book.

> That time of year thou mayst in me behold
> When yellow leaves, or none, or few, do hang
> Upon those boughs which shake against the cold,
> Bare ruin'd choirs, where late the sweet birds sang.

> 5   In me thou see'st the twilight of such day
>   As after sunset fadeth in the west,
>   Which by and by black night doth take away,
>   Death's second self, that seals up all in rest.
>
>   In me thou see'st the glowing of such fire
> 10   That on the ashes of his youth doth lie,
>   As the death-bed whereon it must expire
>   Consum'd with that which it was nourish'd by.
>
>   This thou perceiv'st, which makes thy love more strong,
>   To love that well which thou must leave ere long.

■ Symbol

A great many literary strategies can be seen, in a broad sense, as symbols. Being able to recognize and interpret symbols is a valuable skill for interpreting literary texts.

Symbols are a subset of the general category of metaphor. A symbol is also a comparison between something the author wants the reader to think about and another element, but literary critics do not generally use the terms tenor and vehicle to name the two parts. You can think of the symbol in the same way, though; there is something in the text (basically a tenor) and something to which it is being compared (basically the vehicle). Your job as the reader is to think about the vehicle and identify the characteristics that can be seen to apply to the tenor, the element in the text. In most cases, you will know you are dealing with a symbol rather than a metaphor because the symbol is something which is actually physically present in the text. In the Burns example on page 47, there is no actual rose in the world of the text; the rose is just an idea. If a character in a novel hands another character a rose, however, then that rose might very well be a symbol.

Another important difference between a symbol and a metaphor is that a metaphor is always pointed out directly in the language. The simile uses *like* or *as*, but other metaphors will be equally obvious. In Shakespeare's Sonnet 73 on page 48, for instance, Shakespeare uses the phrase 'That time of year thou mayst in me behold …' as the direct connection between the speaker, 'me', and the 'time of year'. The metaphor is made overt through the language the author uses.

A symbol, on the other hand, requires a leap of interpretation by the reader. Since any object *might* be a symbol, the reader has to be alert to many possibilities. Your first job, then, when working with symbols, is to observe carefully. Take note of any objects, conditions or features of the fabula and then ask yourself if each one might be a symbol. You might have to do some research to find out features of various objects and standard symbolic features of them. In another Carol Ann Duffy poem, 'Ithaca', for instance, she mentions 'turquoise water' (line 7), 'dolphins' (line 13), 'olive trees' (line 15) and 'rosemary' (line 17), among a great many other objects. Most readers would have to do some research to find out that turquoise has traditionally been associated with protection and shielding warriors (Energy Muse), or that dolphins typically symbolize both protection and playfulness (Dolphin Symbolism), or that olive trees are traditional symbols of peace and friendship (Every Olive Tree Has a Story) and so on. As we examine the associations with the objects in the poem, we begin to see a pattern of objects associated with protection, friendship, welcome and peace. The speaker of the poem, it turns out, is returning home after a very long absence, and she is afraid that she will not be welcome. Her seeing all those signs of protection in the environment reveal to the reader her attempt to convince herself that she is in a safe place. They are symbols of her hope. We see into her mental and emotional state and we can appreciate much more deeply the struggle that Duffy is portraying in the figure of her speaker.

The example of 'Ithaca' shows what you need to do as you work on symbols in a literary work. The more work you are willing to do to learn about associations with the objects in a work, the more you are likely to understand and appreciate what the author is doing.

Finally, symbols do not always take their meaning from socially established tradition: authors can create symbols in the context of the work. That process is more likely to occur in a novel than in a poem, because the novel is long enough for a symbol to recur in context several times. In *The Great Gatsby*, for example, F Scott Fitzgerald creates a symbol out of a green light at the end of Daisy Buchanan's dock, which we come to understand is representative of Gatsby's obsession. We don't recognize a green light as being a standard symbol of obsession, but we do have associations with both 'green' and 'light', which help us to understand the nature of Gatsby's desire to possess Daisy. In the beginning of the novel, the light is bright but far away. Later on, as Gatsby actually gets closer to Daisy, the light seems to fade and lose its significance. Fitzgerald uses the light in the context of the novel to make a point about desire and discovering that when we possess what we think we want, it can turn out to be not what we expected. We cannot find that meaning by doing research; we can only get it from reading the novel and paying attention to the details.

If you are reading a novel, short story or play, you cannot do the kind of intensive research into every object in the text that you can do when you are working with a much shorter text such as a poem. In that case, you have to look for indications that something might be important. One way to recognize a symbol in a longer work is by noticing its repetition, as with the green light example in *The Great Gatsby*. Another is to pay attention to objects or elements of the setting that the author spends some time describing. If the author writes a lot of words on something, it is probably more important than something just mentioned in passing. Our first introduction to the green light in *Gatsby*, for example, comes at the end of the first chapter:

> I didn't call to him for he gave a sudden intimation that he was content to be alone—he stretched out his arms toward the dark water in a curious way, and far as I was from him, I could have sworn he was trembling. Involuntarily I glanced seaward—and distinguished nothing except a single green light, minute and far
> 5 away, that might have been at the end of a dock. (25–6)

The light itself is only mentioned once and it is not described other than as *green*, but it is put in a context which gives it a great deal of significance. We are led to believe that it is the sight of the green light which makes Gatsby ['he'] tremble. The light has a powerful effect on the character; the light is, therefore, important. Fitzgerald has signalled to us that the light is a symbol of something but we have to keep reading in order to find out what.

Another way to help you narrow down potential symbols is for you to become familiar with common types of symbols. Here is a partial list of the kinds of symbols you might encounter:

- Weather as symbol.

- Seasons as symbol.

- Setting as symbol.

- Religious symbols.

- Objects as symbols.

- Colours as symbols.

- Standard cultural symbols such as flags or emblematic animals.

These symbols can function in any literary genre – poetry, prose or drama.

■ Weather as a symbol

Weather often serves to indicate characters' feelings or overall tone. Rain often suggests sadness and sunshine, happiness. Rain changing to sunshine might mean an improving situation. Immersion in and arising from water is symbolic of rebirth – baptism – and so we might expect that a character who is soaked in rain might be undergoing some sort of significant change, or rebirth, into a new life or new kind of person. Storms are commonly damaging, so a storm in a work can indicate trouble for the characters. If you think about how weather is used in a text you are studying, you might find that it is a symbol to reveal something about characters or situations.

ACTIVITY 3: 'MASTER HAROLD' ... AND THE BOYS

The play *'Master Harold' ... and the boys* by Athol Fugard begins with a character, Hally, coming in out of the rain and ends with that same character going back out into the storm. Given what you know about how weather can serve as a symbol, comment on what you might find happening with that character. After you have come up with your interpretations, you can read the notes at the end of the book.

■ Seasons as a symbol

The cycle of seasons, like the cycle of a day, is traditionally correlated with the cycle of life and death. That comparison has its roots in the fact that the Earth comes to life, blossoms, fades and dies off each year as the seasons pass. Spring is the season of birth, when plants grow and the air warms. Summer is the season of maturity, when flowers and other plants are at their fullest bloom. Autumn is the season of approaching death, when the leaves turn and fall, and winter, when the earth can be covered in snow and ice, is the season we associate with death. The cycle of the day likewise moves from birth to death in accordance with the passage of the sun. We move from darkness to light and then to darkness again.

ACTIVITY 4: 'THE PRODIGAL' BY ELIZABETH BISHOP

'The Prodigal' is a poem about an alcoholic who has exiled himself from his home and family by his drinking. The poem has two stanzas. The first focuses on how the man (the *prodigal*) feels in the mornings. Even though you have not read the entire poem, you should be able to make some educated guesses, based on common use of symbolism, about what the references to morning and night might suggest about the man in the poem. When you have made your own interpretation, read the notes at the end of the book.

> But sometimes mornings after drinking bouts
> (he hid the pints behind a two-by-four),
> the sunrise glazed the barnyard mud with red;
> the burning puddles seemed to reassure. (lines 9–12)

The second stanza focuses on how he feels at night:

> But evenings the first star came to warn.
> The farmer whom he worked for came at dark ... (lines 15–16)

■ Setting as a symbol

Weather and seasons are obviously features of setting, so those are two ways you can analyse the symbolic function of setting, but there are other ways in which a setting can be symbolic. Settings often involve openings or barriers: walls, towers and closed doors or gates are all barriers. Windows, open doors or gates are all openings. Locks can represent barriers while keys can represent openings. Certain kinds of buildings are familiar symbols: castles are symbolic of royalty and power, as are government buildings such as the US White House or the British Houses of Parliament. Prisons are symbols of entrapment and punishment. Houses are often symbolic of safety and welcome. A run down, decrepit building, on the other hand, can symbolize the loss of any of these things.

Water has many symbolic functions. As mentioned earlier, it often suggests rebirth: if a character emerges from water (a pool, a rain shower, a lake – or any other body of water), you should consider whether that character is in some way changed. Water can also be a barrier that must be crossed (think of the biblical story of the parting of the Red Sea). Water can symbolize death, as in drowning, and frozen water can also be a sign of death, because of its associations with winter. Storms can symbolize trouble, and, by extension, rainbows can symbolize hope for the future. Rainbows are also religious symbols: according to the Christian Bible, God sent a rainbow after the great flood as a sign of hope for the future and a promise that he would never again destroy nearly all of creation.

Finally, characters are often seen in relation to each other by where they are situated in the setting. If one character is physically higher up in the setting than another (at the top of a staircase, for example), that character might be seen to have more authority or social status than the other. If a character is moving up – climbing – that character might be moving up in society, while a character who is physically coming down might be losing strength or status.

■ Example: 'The Fish' by Elizabeth Bishop

One example of the symbolic function of setting comes from 'The Fish' by Elizabeth Bishop. In this poem, the speaker is a fisherwoman who is telling the story of a fish she caught and, ultimately, let go. Look at these two short excerpts:

> I caught a tremendous fish
> and held him beside the boat
> half out of water, with my hook
> fast in a corner of his mouth. (lines 1–4)
>
> ...– until everything
> was rainbow, rainbow, rainbow!
> And I let the fish go. (lines 77–9)

We see in the first extract that the fish has emerged from water. Usually, emergence from water suggests rebirth, but we must think for a minute: if a fish emerges from water, it dies.

KEY TERM

Irony – using words or phrases to convey an intended meaning different from the literal meaning, or in contrast to the expected meaning.

So, in this case, the symbol is **ironic**; Bishop has inverted our expectations. That reading is confirmed when we get to the end of the poem in the second extract. The fisherwoman let the fish go – back into the water, back to what might be seen as a new chance at life. The rainbow is also a symbol here: the rainbow seems to have reminded the fisherwoman of God's mercy, and so she was also merciful. We can speculate that there is a cause/effect relationship because of that *and*: when the fisherwoman saw the rainbow, she decided to let the fish go.

The possibilities for how elements of the setting might function symbolically are endless. Your job as a reader is to notice the details of the setting, think about the associations we have with various elements of setting, and then ask yourself whether the author intends us to recognize those features as symbols. If you can make a logical association, then you can be pretty sure that the symbolic meaning was intended.

ACTIVITY 5: 'MOTHER TO SON' BY LANGSTON HUGHES

Read the poem and consider the various elements of the setting that Hughes has named. Decide how the setting works symbolically and explain your thinking for each element of setting. There are notes at the end of the book, but you should try your own interpretation before reading those.

> Well, son, I'll tell you:
> Life for me ain't been no crystal stair.
> It's had tacks in it,
> And splinters,
> 5 And boards torn up,
> And places with no carpet on the floor—
> Bare.
> But all the time
> I'se been a-climbin' on,
> 10 And reachin' landin's,
> And turnin' corners,
> And sometimes goin' in the dark
> Where there ain't been no light.
> So boy, don't you turn back.
> 15 Don't you set down on the steps
> 'Cause you finds it's kinder hard.
> Don't you fall now—
> For I'se still goin', honey,
> I'se still climbin',
> 20 And life for me ain't been no crystal stair.

■ Religious symbols

We have already noted the rainbow as a religious symbol in the last section; there are many more. The fish is a symbol of the Messiah in Christianity, for example.

Some of the most common religious symbols that you will encounter in Western literature are those related to the Christian story of the Garden of Eden. In that story, Adam and Eve were created to live in the Garden of Eden, which was a paradise. They were told they could eat of any plants they wanted, with one exception: they were not to eat the fruit of the tree of knowledge. A serpent came along, however, and tempted Eve to eat the fruit.

She did so and also gave some to Adam. They became aware of their own nakedness and tried to cover it. God thus knew that they had disobeyed him, and he expelled them from Eden. As part of the punishment, according to Christian doctrine, men were destined to have to earn their living by labouring, and women were destined forever to suffer pain in child bearing. This event is called the fall from grace.

Any time you come across the mention of a tree or a garden, you should definitely consider whether the author is expecting you to recognize the religious allusion and whether, therefore, those elements are symbolic. If you encounter a mention of fruit, or of an apple, that is also very likely to be symbolic of the Garden of Eden story. Note that the Bible refers to the fruit of the tree of knowledge – not apples – but apples became associated with the story in the fourth century. The extract below explains why this happened.

■ Example: *In Defense of Puns* by James Geary

> … that's when Pope Damasus I asked Saint Jerome to translate the Old Latin Bible into the simpler Latin Vulgate, which became the definitive edition of the text for the next thousand years. In the Vulgate, the adjectival form of *evil*, *malus*, is *malum*, which also happens to be the word for 'apple'. The similarity between *malum* ('evil') and *malum* ('apple') prompted Saint Jerome to pick that word to describe what Eve and Adam ate, thereby ushering sin into the world. (30)

The mention of any fruit, however, might be a symbol of temptation to evil. The myth of Persephone pre-figures the Christian story, and the fruit that Persephone ate, which tied her permanently to Hades, was a pomegranate.

Another very common Christian symbol is the symbol of the Madonna and child – Mary and her baby, Jesus. Mary, the virgin, was chosen to be the mother of God's son, and so the Madonna is a symbol of goodness and purity. Any time you encounter an image of a mother with a baby, you should ask yourself whether it is a symbol of the Madonna.

In the short story 'Everything That Rises Must Converge' by Flannery O'Connor, we find two pairs of mothers and sons. The first is a white woman with a grown son, who has accompanied her to a class at the Y because the mother's doctor has ordered her to lose weight to improve her health, and the second is an African American woman with a young son. The latter get on the bus and sit down next to the first mother and son. (Note that African American characters are called *negro* in the story because of the time period when it was written. You will remember the discussion of context of production and interpretation in Chapter 2 – the same concepts function with the interpretation of literary works, so you will often need to do some research to understand the context of the work.)

■ Example: 'Everything That Rises Must Converge' by Flannery O'Connor

> He [the grown son] was tilted out of his fantasy again as the bus stopped. The door opened with a sucking hiss and out of the dark a large, gaily dressed, sullen-looking colored woman got on with a little boy. The child, who might have been four, had on a short plaid suit and a Tyrolean hat with a blue feather in it. Julian hoped
> 5 that he would sit down beside him and that the woman would push in beside his mother. He could think of no better arrangement.

> As she waited for her tokens, the woman was surveying the seating possibilities—
> he hoped with the idea of sitting where she was least wanted. There was
> something familiar-looking about her but Julian could not place what it was. She
> 10 was a giant of a woman. Her face was set not only to meet opposition but to seek
> it out. The downward tilt of her large lower lip was like a warning sign: DON'T
> TAMPER WITH ME. Her bulging figure was encased in a green crepe dress and her
> feet overflowed in red shoes. She had on a hideous hat. A purple velvet flap came
> down on one side of it and stood up on the other; the rest of it was green and
> 15 looked like a cushion with the stuffing out. She carried a mammoth red pocketbook
> that bulged throughout as if it were stuffed with rocks.
>
> To Julian's disappointment, the little boy climbed up on the empty seat beside
> his mother. His mother lumped all children, black and white, into the common
> category, 'cute,' and she thought little Negroes were on the whole cuter than little
> 20 white children. She smiled at the little boy as he climbed on the seat.
>
> Meanwhile the woman was bearing down upon the empty seat beside Julian. To
> his annoyance, she squeezed herself into it. He saw his mother's face change as the
> woman settled herself next to him and he realized with satisfaction that this was
> more objectionable to her than it was to him. (15–16)

In this passage, we see that the white mother with her son is not a traditional symbol of the Madonna, but she might be an ironic symbol. We know she is not well, and physical ill-health often signifies a kind of illness of personality. This woman is angered by the arrival of the African Americans – she is obviously bigoted and concerned about her son being somehow contaminated. We see her as an unpleasant and un-Christian character. By contrast, the other woman with her little boy are depicted as more positive. They are obviously not concerned with the race of their fellow passengers, and the little boy is depicted in a colourful suit and a hat with a feather (possibly a hint there of a bird, a sign of freedom). The contrasting Madonna figures help to make a point about the ugliness of racism.

The religious symbols we have investigated here are typical in Western literature, but you may encounter some allusions to other religions. If you are reading a text set in a Muslim, Hindu or other religious culture, you may have to do some research to find out what religious allusions there are. You should approach the task the same way you've done all the others: read carefully, observe closely. Take note of what objects are mentioned and do some research to find out what they might signify.

Finally, note the overlap between the allusions and the symbols. Very often when you encounter a religious, historical or literary allusion, it has been used in order to function symbolically.

ACTIVITY 6: 'ADAM CAST FORTH' BY JORGE LUIS BORGES

We know from the title that this poem is going to allude to the story of the Garden of Eden. Read the poem and see if you can find some ways in which Borges has used symbols related to the Garden of Eden. Make a list and explain their significance. After you are done, read the notes at the end of the book.

Note: Borges wrote in Spanish, so this version is a translation. Be aware that your interpretation of this work is of a translation, which might differ in significant ways from the original.

> Was there a Garden or was the Garden a dream?
> Amid the fleeting light, I have slowed myself and queried,
> Almost for consolation, if the bygone period
> Over which this Adam, wretched now, once reigned supreme,
> 5   Might not have been just a magical illusion
> Of that God I dreamed. Already it's imprecise
> In my memory, the clear Paradise,
> But I know it exists, in flower and profusion,
> Although not for me. My punishment for life
> 10   Is the stubborn earth with the incestuous strife
> Of Cains and Abels and their brood; I await no pardon.
> Yet, it's much to have loved, to have known true joy,
> To have had – if only for just one day –
> The experience of touching the living Garden.

◼ Objects, colours and standard symbols

We looked earlier at some examples of objects as symbols when we considered the green light in F Scott Fitzgerald's novel, the fish in Elizabeth Bishop's poem, and the staircase in Langston Hughes' poem. In some of those cases, we were considering the objects under some categories of symbols (context, setting, etc.). Those categories help you to recognize particular kinds of symbols and point you to a different meaning you might find, but remember that almost any object can be a symbol, whether it fits into a category named here or not.

Any time you encounter an object which seems to have some prominence in a literary text, you can think about it in terms of whether it might have a symbolic function. Consider what you know about that object in the real world, and then ask yourself whether those features help you to understand the object in the text.

A broom, for instance, might be a sign of something that needs to be, or is being, cleaned up. A loaf of bread might be a symbol of nurturing. It might even be a religious symbol, referring to the Christian association with Jesus as the bread of life. Bread is used in the communion ceremony to symbolize the nurturing Christians get from their belief in Jesus. A car can be a symbol of a journey, which in turn can be a symbol of a character embarking on an adventure that leads them to change in fundamental ways. A sports car could symbolize power and recklessness, while a stodgy old sedan might symbolize someone who lacks a sense of adventure and is rather boring. Animals can be symbols too: tigers suggest strength and stealth; rabbits signify something gentle and timid. Cats might symbolize gods or lazy creatures or independence, while dogs might symbolize loyalty.

Colours very often have a symbolic function. Lots of colours have quite a wide variety of symbolic meanings. We are accustomed to thinking of gold and silver as colours symbolizing riches, red as a common symbol either for love or for blood and death, and black as symbolizing darkness and evil. Colour symbolism, however, is culture-dependent: in many western cultures, for example, white is worn at weddings, because it is a symbol of purity. In Japan, however, white is a symbol of mourning, and red is worn at weddings. One reason the rainbow is a symbol of hope is that it entails all colours, and so suggests unity.

The final type of symbol that we will consider here are standard symbols, which are established by communities and have set meanings. Here are some standard symbols that you will probably recognize:

If you find a standard symbol described in a literary work, then you will be able to tell from the context if you should employ the standard meaning. An eagle in the woods, for example, might be a more general symbol for you to interpret, but an eagle in a photo on the wall of a character who is a corrupt politician would be interpreted as a standard symbol of power – possibly used ironically.

With the exception of standard symbols, the important thing for you to remember is that there are no rules for how to interpret objects as symbols. All the examples we just went through are possibilities, rather than certainties. You must read about the object in context and then call on your knowledge of the characteristics of the important objects to decide what meaning makes sense. This kind of interpretive work is part of what makes reading fun – you, the reader, have a real role to play in divining the meaning. You are not merely a passive participant being told what to think; you get to engage in the creative effort.

ACTIVITY 7: 'LEGEND' BY JUDITH WRIGHT

This is the first stanza of Australian poet Judith Wright's poem, 'Legend'. Using what you have learned about symbols in this chapter, try to locate and interpret as many symbols as you possibly can. Make a list of the symbols and write down your explanations of what you think they might mean. When you are done, you can read the notes at the end of the book.

> The blacksmith's boy went out with a rifle
> and a black dog running behind.
> Cobwebs snatched at his feet,
> rivers hindered him,
> 5   thorn branches caught at his eyes to make him blind
> and the sky turned into an unlucky opal,
> but he didn't mind.
> I can break branches, I can swim rivers, I can stare out
> any spider I meet,
> 10 said he to his dog and his rifle.

Structure

Structure refers to how a work is organized. Often a good reader will identify the structure of a work and then use it in order to help understand what the author is trying to convey. Works of different literary forms tend to rely on different types of structure and structural elements, but in all forms, you can use the structure to help you understand what the author is trying to accomplish.

■ The structure of novels

A novel is usually structured into chapters. Your job is to try to figure out why the chapters are ordered in the way they are and why the novelist decided to divide the chapters up in that way. Sometimes chapters are divided among different narrators. *The Thirteenth Tale*, by Diane Setterfield, uses two narrators, one of whom is telling the story of her life to another.

The chapters take us through the past and present life of the listening narrator, Margaret Lea, and through the past life of the second narrator, Vida Winter. Authors may also organize the chapters by switching among stories of different characters. *Before the Fall*, by Noah Hawley, is divided into chapters in this way. The novel centres around an investigation of a plane crash that killed nine people, and the chapters trace the threads of the past life of each person on the plane, interwoven with chapters that follow the investigation of the crash. Chapters can also be divided by different time periods. The method of interweaving present-day events with flashbacks is fairly common. You can see it in *The Book of Speculation* by Erika Swyler and in *Little Fires Everywhere* by Celeste Ng. In each case, the authors work gradually to converge two story lines. The technique often helps build suspense.

Another common method of organizing a novel is to have the action move from place to place. *Persuasion*, by Jane Austen, begins at two different country estates, then moves to Lyme Regis, then moves to Bath. Your job as a reader is to figure out what the changes in place mean. You may have heard of the 'Hero's Journey'; that is a model that describes how heroic characters change (or fail to change) over the course of their experiences. Whenever you see any mention of travelling or a journey, you should be alert to how the adventures encountered on the journey change the character – for better or for worse – as he or she moves from place to place. In the case of *Persuasion*, the heroine, Anne Elliot, develops strength of character as she travels, and her would-be lover, a man to whom she was engaged eight years previously, but who she broke up with on the advice of friends, begins to learn to trust her again. A good reader will examine the events and characteristics of each place and notice how they reflect the changes in the characters.

The most common kind of structural element in narrative fiction is the plot. A plot is a series of events which are linked causally. One event causes the next event, which causes the next event, which causes the next event and so on. If you identify the cause–effect relationships between events in novels, you will be able to understand the characters' thinking and motivations, which will, in turn, help you to understand what the author is trying to reveal about human nature and human experience.

Short stories might have chapters or chapter-like breaks, but the use of those structural elements is not very common. All the other kinds of structural elements that exist in novels may be used in short stories, however, so work on interpreting them the same way: look for cause–effect events, changes of location or identifiable sections that you can name.

The following is the opening of Katherine Mansfield's short story 'The Garden Party'.

■ Example: 'The Garden Party' by Katherine Mansfield

They could not have had a more perfect day for a garden-party if they had ordered it. Windless, warm, the sky without a cloud. Only the blue was veiled with a haze of light gold, as it is sometimes in early summer. The gardener had been up since dawn, mowing the lawns and sweeping them, until the grass and the dark flat
5 rosettes where the daisy plants had been seemed to shine. As for the roses, you could not help feeling they understood that roses are the only flowers that impress people at garden-parties; the only flowers that everybody is certain of knowing. Hundreds, yes, literally hundreds, had come out in a single night; the green bushes bowed down as though they had been visited by archangels.

10 Breakfast was not yet over before the men came to put up the marquee.

> 'Where do you want the marquee put, mother?'
>
> 'My dear child, it's no use asking me. I'm determined to leave everything to you children this year. Forget I am your mother. Treat me as an honoured guest.'
>
> 15   But Meg could not possibly go and supervise the men. She had washed her hair before breakfast, and she sat drinking her coffee in a green turban, with a dark wet curl stamped on each cheek. Jose, the butterfly, always came down in a silk petticoat and a kimono jacket.
>
> 'You'll have to go, Laura; you're the artistic one.'
>
> Away Laura flew, still holding her piece of bread-and-butter. It's so delicious to have
> 20   an excuse for eating out of doors, and besides, she loved having to arrange things; she always felt she could do it so much better than anybody else.

We can consider how this extract is organized in at least two different ways: we can look at plot, the causal relationship between events, and we can look at the order in which Mansfield has chosen to have the narrator tell the events.

The passage begins with a long paragraph of description (lines 1–9), and then shifts to dialogue between a daughter and a mother (lines 11–13). We are then introduced to two other daughters. The mother and the first two daughters all reject responsibility for organizing the men putting up the marquee (lines 12–17). In the final section, one of the sisters assigns the job to the final sister, Laura, and Laura willingly takes on the task. If we think about those sections in terms of what we are learning about the situation, we can see that in the opening paragraph, we have a portrait of a garden scene which is the result of a lot of hard work on the part of the gardener. In the middle section, that portrait is contrasted by an introduction to three women who do not work – who want to be pampered. The passage ends with a daughter who, in sharp contrast, eagerly embraces the work that awaits her. Through this organization, Mansfield has begun to introduce us to the nature of her characters. The mother and the first two daughters are similar to the flowers in the setting, while the final daughter is more like the gardener.

We can consider the same passage from the perspective of the cause–effect relationship among the events. In this case, we see that the gardener's hard work has resulted in the garden being in pristine condition. The arrival of the men with the marquee causes the conversation between the mother and the first daughter, Meg. The mother's refusal to deal with the men causes a need for someone else to do it. The refusal of Meg and Jose to take care of it leads to Laura being ordered to do it. From that sequence of events, we see how powerful a motivator denial is in this opening passage. Laura, by contrast, is a person who takes action.

Either one of those methods of analysing the structure helps us to understand something important that Mansfield is trying to show us about her characters.

■ The structure of drama

We considered how the structure of a prose work can contribute to meaning; the same is even more true with drama. As a starting point, drama has a structure that consists of the components described below.

■ Opening balance

The opening balance is the situation in the fictional world at the beginning of the play. People might not be happy, but there is a status quo to which the characters have been

KEY TERM

Opening balance – the situation in the fictional world at the beginning of a play.

accustomed. In *Romeo and Juliet*, for example, the opening balance is a situation in which the two families, Capulet and Montague, have been feuding for some time and in which Prince Escalus has decreed that the fighting in the streets must stop.

■ Disturbance

A **disturbance** occurs when something happens to upset the balance and force the characters to deal with an unexpected problem. The Capulet and Montague servants open the play by starting a fight, in defiance of the prince's order.

■ Protagonist

The protagonist is the character who has the plan for dealing with the disturbance. The plan should have two important aspects:

- An objective which is the resolution of the problem.
- Steps to be taken.

Prince Escalus is the **protagonist** here: he tries to stop the fighting permanently by threatening to have anyone who starts another fight killed. His plan, therefore, is to use that threat and the steps he takes are to announce the threat, then to meet with the heads of the families to ensure that they understand him. (Note that this is surprising; many people would likely think of Romeo as the protagonist in this play, but the Romeo and Juliet love story is actually a second plot, and not the one that opens the play.)

■ Antagonist

Not every play has an **antagonist**, but many do. An antagonist is a character who is working consciously to stop the protagonist from implementing his or her plan. In *Romeo and Juliet*, it is debatable whether or not there is an antagonist: we could say that Tybalt, who starts the next fight, is antagonistic to the prince's plan. However, he does so in the heat of anger, and not specifically in order to defy the prince.

■ Obstacles

An **obstacle** is something that already exists in the fictional situation, the fabula, which interferes with the protagonist's ability to implement the plan. There might be one or more obstacles. An obstacle to Prince Escalus' plan is the hatred that the two families have for each other – and especially Tybalt's hatred for Romeo. That hatred existed before the prince implemented his plan, so it is an obstacle, rather than a complication.

■ Complications

A **complication** is something that arises as a result of the protagonist's effort to implement the plan, and which interferes with the ability to employ the plan effectively. A complication that arises in *Romeo and Juliet* is that when it is time for the prince to order the consequence he promised, he cannot do so, as it was Mercutio, his own relative, who killed Tybalt in defiance of the order not to fight. Romeo is therefore banished, instead of killed.

■ Climax

The **climax** is the final complication that determines whether the plan is going to be successful or not. If the climax can be dealt with effectively, the plan will succeed. If it cannot, the plan will fail. There is an interesting question with *Romeo and Juliet*, as to what we might call the climax. The puzzle for the audience arises because Shakespeare deftly weaves the second plot, the love and death of Romeo and Juliet, into the first plot: the feud. As we eventually find out, the feud ends when Romeo and Juliet kill themselves, so we can say that the climax is the scene in the tomb during which that happens. That is the action which directly causes the end of the feud, which is what the prince initially wanted. Ironically, his plan was not the reason for his goal being met.

■ Resolution

The **resolution** is the outcome and brings a new balance. If the plan ultimately succeeds in solving the problem, then we are likely to have a happy ending. If the plan does not solve the problem, we are likely to have an unhappy ending. Keep in mind, however, that the protagonist might have had a bad plan – in that case, even if the plan succeeded then the ending might, ironically, be unhappy. In *Romeo and Juliet*, given that the initial disturbance was the literal disturbance of the peace on the streets of Verona because the feud between the Capulets and Montagues broke out again, we know that we have a final resolution (apparently) of the end of the feud in the wake of the deaths of Romeo and Juliet. The families reconcile and promise to honour their children.

■ Conflict and suspense

Two other elements of structure that you are likely to find in a drama are **conflict** and **suspense**. Conflict can arise almost anywhere – it might be conflict between the protagonist and the antagonist, it might be part of the complications that arise from the effort to implement the plan, or a major conflict might even provide the climax. The conflict might be internal to the protagonist as well; it does not have to be a conflict between two different characters. In *Romeo and Juliet*, the many conflicts are famous: the feud between the two families, the conflict between Tybalt and Romeo, the conflict between the prince and the families, the conflict between the servants, and so on.

Suspense arises when the playwright keeps the audience waiting to see what will happen next, and, like conflict, it can occur at various places throughout a play. Every time a problem arises, whether it be the disturbance, an obstacle or a complication, and we don't know that the outcome is inevitable, we have suspense. Probably the greatest moment of suspense in *Romeo and Juliet* is the moment during which Romeo is observing Juliet's apparently-dead body and is about to kill himself. The audience knows that she is not dead, and that moment of **dramatic irony** provides suspense.

■ Departure from the basic structure

The elements of dramatic structure which are detailed in the previous section are what might be considered standard elements. The fun for a playwright and for the audience, however, is to begin with that basic structure and then manipulate it to create a certain effect. We have already seen some hints of variation from the basic plot structure in the brief examples from *Romeo and Juliet* in the section above.

One of the most common variations on that standard structure is the inclusion of subplots, each one with its own structure – balance, disturbance, protagonist, and so on. Shakespeare's plays always feature at least one important subplot which offers a different version of the main plot. In *The Taming of the Shrew*, for instance, the main plot features the problem of the marriageability of Katherine, the shrew, who battles with Petruchio even after they are married. But there is also a strong subplot that features her sister, Bianca, who appears to be a much better marriage prospect than Katherine, but who turns out to be a problem in her own right.

■ Structure in poetry

Poetry differs from other genres of literary texts in that poets use several recognized and standardized structures. Not all poems have a formal structure, but many do. You may be familiar with the sonnet structure, as in Shakespeare's Sonnet 73, which we looked at earlier in the chapter. This is a classic Shakespearean sonnet, with three quatrains followed by a **couplet**. The **rhyme** scheme is 'abab', 'cdcd', 'efef', 'gg', as shown:

KEY TERMS

Resolution – in drama, the outcome that brings a new balance.

Conflict – a struggle between two opposing forces.

Suspense – a feeling from the audience when waiting for an outcome.

KEY TERMS

Dramatic irony – when the audience knows something that the characters in the play do not.

Couplet – two lines in a poem that typically rhyme and are of the same length and metre.

Rhyme – the repetition of two or more similar sounds, often occurring at the ends of a line in poetry.

KEY TERMS

Villanelle – a poem of 19 lines, with only two rhymes throughout, and some lines repeated.

Sestina – a complex verse form with six stanzas of six lines and a final triplet. All stanzas have the same six words at the line ends in six different sequences. The final triplet contains all six words.

Ode – a lyrical poem usually without a regular metre.

Ballad – a poem of short stanzas that narrates a story, often arranged in quatrains.

Petrarchan sonnet – a sonnet consisting of an octet followed by a sestet – eight lines followed by six lines. The rhyme scheme is 'abba', 'abba', 'cde', 'cde'. You will see several variations of the 'cde' rhymes, however.

Octet – an eight-line stanza.

Sestet – a six-line stanza.

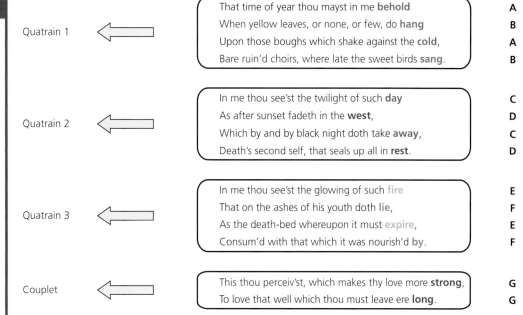

Quatrain 1
```
That time of year thou mayst in me behold          A
When yellow leaves, or none, or few, do hang       B
Upon those boughs which shake against the cold,    A
Bare ruin'd choirs, where late the sweet birds sang. B
```

Quatrain 2
```
In me thou see'st the twilight of such day         C
As after sunset fadeth in the west,                D
Which by and by black night doth take away,        C
Death's second self, that seals up all in rest.    D
```

Quatrain 3
```
In me thou see'st the glowing of such fire         E
That on the ashes of his youth doth lie,           F
As the death-bed whereupon it must expire,         E
Consum'd with that which it was nourish'd by.      F
```

Couplet
```
This thou perceiv'st, which makes thy love more strong, G
To love that well which thou must leave ere long.  G
```

Some other formal poetic structures include the **villanelle**, the **sestina**, the **ode** and the **ballad**. We do not have space in this chapter to investigate all or even a few of the formal poetic structures to which poets often turn. You should, however, be aware that they exist, and when you do read a poem with one of the formal structures, make sure that you educate yourself as to the *rules* of that form. What is important to notice is any variation of those rules and then to ask yourself what that variation suggests in terms of meaning.

In her poem, 'Demeter', for example, Carol Ann Duffy uses a basic **Petrarchan sonnet**, a form that normally uses an **octet** (an eight-line unit) followed by a **sestet** (a six-line unit) but she inverts it, so that the sestet comes first. If you look at the sonnet closely, you will see that in the sestet, the speaker is sad and lonely, but in the octet, which describes the return of her daughter, the mood turns to joy. The inversion of the form suggests the weight of the joy which outweighs the initial sorrow.

■ Example: 'Demeter' by Carol Ann Duffy

```
Where I lived – winter and hard earth.
I sat in my cold stone room
choosing tough words, granite flint,

to break the ice. My broken heart –
I tried that, but it skimmed,
flat, over the frozen lake.

She came from a long, long way,
but I saw her at last, walking,
my daughter, my girl, across the fields,

in bare feet, bringing all spring's flowers
to her mother's house. I swear
the air softened and warmed as she moved,

the blue sky smiling, none too soon,
with the small shy mouth of a new moon.
```

Sestet: we know that these six lines go together because of the volta. A volta is a significant turn in the direction of the poem. The focus changes between stanzas two and three from the mother's experience while the daughter is gone to the daughter's return.

Octet: This structure has been inverted from the usual octet followed by sestet.

Some poetry, however, does not conform to any recognized formal structure. Such poetry is called **free verse**. When studying poetry, do not make the mistake of thinking that a free verse poem does not have any structure. You just have to look at how the content of the poem is structured, just as you would look at how content can be used to structure prose. If we look at 'Birth of the Owl Butterflies' by Ruth Sharman, for example, we can immediately see some elements of structure which do not arise from either **metre** or formal poetic structure.

■ Example: 'Birth of the Owl Butterflies' by Ruth Sharman

> They hung in our kitchen for days:
> a row of brown lanterns that threw no light,
> merely darkened with their growing load.
> Pinned to a shelf among the knick-knacks
> 5 and the cookery books;
> ripening in the radiator's heat:
> six Central American *Caligo* chrysalids,
> five thousand miles from their mountain home.
>
> My father had brought them here,
> 10 carefully packed in cotton wool,
> to hatch, set, identify, and display:
> these unpromising dingy shells plumped up
> like curled leaves, on each a silver spur,
> a tiny gleam or drop of dew
> 15 Nature had added as a finishing touch
> to perfect mimicry.
>
> For weeks the wizened fruit had been maturing.
> Now, one by one, the pods exploded,
> crackling in the quiet kitchen,
> 20 and a furry missile emerged – quickly,
> as if desperate to break free –
> unhinged its awkward legs,
> hauling behind it, like a frilly party dress,
> the rumpled mass of its soft wings.
>
> 25 It clung unsteadily to the cloven pod,
> while slow wings billowed with the blood
> that pumped them full.
> The dark velvet began to glow
> with a thousand tiny striations,
> 30 and there, in each corner,
> boldly ringed in black and gold,
> two fierce owl-eyes widened.
>
> Uneasy minutes, these, before *Caligo*
> can flex its nine-inch wings and fly.
> 35 They drooped still, gathering strength,

> limp flags loosely flowing.
> When two butterflies hatched too close,
> and clashed, each scrabbling for a footing,
> one fell and its wings flopped
> 40 fatly on the kitchen floor.
>
> I pictured them shattering later
> on taps and cupboard corners;
> but my father gauged his moment well,
> allowed a first few timid forays,
> 45 then swooped down gentle-fingered
> with his glass jar for the kill.
> The monstrous wings all but filled it,
> beat vigorously, fluttered, and were still.

We can see right away, for instance, that there are six stanzas of eight lines each – six octets. We don't have a named structure for such a poem, but we might take a guess about why the poet chose it. For one thing, the poem is about six butterflies, so in a way, there is one octet per butterfly. Beyond that, we can look at what is happening in each stanza, possibly in terms of the actions in the fabula (the fictional world), but also, and more interestingly, in terms of what the speaker is doing in each octet. If we look at the literal events, we can see that they break down as follows:

KEY TERMS

Dramatic situation – the situation in which the events of the story happen.

Narrative situation – the situation in which the narrator tells the story.

Stanza	What is happening in the **dramatic situation?**
1	The chrysalids have not hatched; they've **been brought** to the speaker's home and were **waiting** to hatch.
2	Nothing new happens here; there is a description of a close view of the chrysalids and a comparison of them to water on a leaf.
3	The butterflies **hatch** and start **trying to move**, which is difficult considering the load of their folded wings.
4	One butterfly's wings **begin to spread and dry**. Description again of a close view.
5	Minutes **pass** while the wings dry. Wings **begin** to **strengthen** and **spread**. Two butterflies **crash** into each other and one falls on the floor.
6	The speaker **imagines** what would inevitably happen to the butterflies if they **started flying** around the kitchen. The father **swoops** down and **catches** the first of the butterflies in the killing jar and it **dies**.

If we consider those events in terms of a structure, we can see that the first two stanzas cover the time period in which the butterflies were transported and awaited hatching. The butterflies hatch in stanza three, and then for three stanzas the wings dry and the butterflies fumble around. In the final stanza, the father kills the butterflies. The poem is structured chronologically, but the focus on events is not spread out equally. There is much more attention on the birth and relatively short life of the butterflies.

This observation already points us to something that the speaker is doing with time: she compresses time in the beginning, zooms in in the middle, and then cuts it off abruptly at the end, which is, of course, what death does at the end of a life.

Now let's look at what's happening in the **narrative situation** – what the speaker is doing in terms of building her story.

Stanza	What is the speaker doing to construct her text?
1	The whole story is a flashback; the narrator here **remembers** the butterfly chrysalids hanging in the kitchen. She **contrasts** the kitchen to the butterflies' natural habitat 5 000 miles away.
2	The speaker **explains** her father's actions and motivations in bringing the butterflies home, and she describes the chrysalids in detail.
3	The speaker **moves the story ahead in time** to the day when the butterflies hatch. She **tells** us that weeks passed between their arrival in the kitchen and their hatching. She **describes** the hatching in detail, as well as the newly hatched butterfly.
4	She **describes** in detail the unfurling of the drying wings. Time has slowed down; the previous stanza covered weeks, this one covers moments.
5	The speaker **describes** the next few minutes while the butterflies' wings open. She **describes** the crash between two butterflies who were too close together.
6	The narrator **reports** her thoughts in the moment that the butterflies became able to fly, and then she **describes** her father catching and killing the first butterfly. We are left to imagine that he did the same to all the rest.

Notice how the highlighted verbs are all actions that a person takes when talking or writing about something. Contrast those to the highlighted verbs in the first table; those are actions that people, and in this case butterflies, can take in the real world.

We can see that the main strategy the narrator uses is description, as opposed to talking about her responses to what she sees. She observes, and imagines, the butterflies in an environment entirely alien to them. Structurally, we have already noted that she adjusts her use of time to create an intense focus on the very short lives of the butterflies. That strategy heightens the shock at the end when the butterflies, just at the very moment when those wings are fully open and can fly, are killed.

In this poem, we have found that a primary structural device is the use of time, and it helps us understand that the narrator and, by implication, the poet, is making a comment about human power over fragile nature and raises the question of whether it is morally acceptable for us to cut lives so very abruptly short.

ACTIVITY 8: STRUCTURE IN LORNA GOODISON'S 'FAREWELL WILD WOMAN (I)'

Read the following poem 'Farewell Wild Woman (I)' by Lorna Goodison and consider how it is structured. Make sure first that you understand what is literally happening, and then consider how the speaker has structured her text. Your verbs should be verbs that have to do with telling: describe, compare, contrast, analyse and so on. Finally, once you have discovered a structure, consider what it might contribute to your understanding of what the poem means. When you are finished, you can review the notes at the end of the book.

> I seemed to have put distance
> between me and the wild woman
> she being certified bad company.
> Always inviting me to drink
> 5 bloody wine from clay cups
> and succumb to false promise
> in the eyes of slim dark men.
> Sometimes though when I'm
> closing the house down early
> 10 and feeling virtuous for living

one more day without falling too low
I think I see her behind the hibiscus
in dresses competing with their red,
and she's spinning a key hung on a
15 cat's eye ring
and inviting me to go low riding.

■ Metre and rhyme as elements of structure

In poetry, metre and rhyme can play very significant roles in conveying meaning. For now, we will just say that metre and rhyme make poetry (and some plays, such as those by Shakespeare) different from other literary forms because they shape the sound of the work. Metre necessarily emphasizes certain words and therefore ideas, and rhyme can do the same thing. The musicality of the text, shaped by the metre and rhyme, will also affect meaning because the sounds of the words – especially at line endings and where the syllables are stressed – will convey a mood to the sensitive reader. Sounds might be harsh or mellifluous (a word which sounds something like what it means: musical and pleasant to listen to). We do not have space in this one chapter to go into the analysis of either of those features, but you should be aware that they are important and, when you have an opportunity to do so, explore them in depth.

ACTIVITY 9: 'UNREADY TO WEAR' BY KURT VONNEGUT, JR

Read the following passage from 'Unready to Wear' by Kurt Vonnegut, Jr and interpret it using all the skills you have learned in this chapter. You should be considering the role of the narrator, the nature of symbols and metaphors, and the structure. Write down your ideas, and then you can refer to the notes at the end of the book.

Whenever it's my turn to get into a body and work as an attendant at the local storage center, I realize all over again how much tougher it is for women to get used to being amphibious.

Madge borrows bodies a lot oftener than I do, and that's true of women in general. We have
5 to keep three times as many women's bodies in stock as men's bodies, in order to meet the demand. Every so often, it seems as though a woman just *has* to have a body, and doll it up in clothes, and look at herself in a mirror. And Madge, God bless her, I don't think she'll be satisfied until she's tried on every body in every storage center on Earth.

It's been a fine thing for Madge, though. I never kid her about it, because it's done so much
10 for her personality. Her old body, to tell you the plain blunt truth, wasn't anything to get excited about, and having to haul the thing around made her gloomy a lot of the time in the old days. She couldn't help it, poor soul, any more than anybody else could help what sort of body they'd been born with, and I loved her in spite of it.

Well, after we'd learned to be amphibious, and after we'd built the storage centers and laid
15 in body supplies and opened them to the public, Madge went hog wild. She borrowed a platinum blonde body that had been donated by a burlesque queen, and I didn't think we'd ever get her out of it. As I say, it did wonders for her self-confidence.

I'm like most men and don't care particularly what body I get. Just the strong, good-looking, healthy bodies were put in storage, one is as good as the next one. Sometimes, when Madge
20 and I take bodies out together for old times' sake, I let her pick out one for me to match whatever she's got on. It's a funny thing how she always picks a blond, tall one for me.

My old body, which she claims she loved for a third of a century, had black hair, and was short and paunchy, too, there toward the last. I'm human and I couldn't help being hurt when they scrapped it after I'd left it, instead of putting it in storage. It was a good, horny,
25 comfortable body; nothing fast and flashy, but reliable. But there isn't much call for that kind of body at the centers, I guess. I never ask for one, at any rate.

30

The worst experience I ever had with a body was when I was flimflammed into taking out the one that had belonged to Dr. Ellis Konigswasser. It belongs to the Amphibious Pioneers' Society and only gets taken out once a year, but for the big Pioneers' Day Parade, on the anniversary of Konigswasser's discovery. Everybody said it was a great honor for me to be picked to get into Konigswasser's body and lead the parade.

35

Like a plain damn fool, I believed them. They'll have a tough time getting me into that thing again – ever. Taking that wreck out certainly made it plain why Konigswasser discovered how people could do without their bodies. That old one of his practically *drives* you out. Ulcers, headaches, arthritis, fallen arches – a nose like a pruning hook, piggy little Y and a complexion like a used steamer trunk. He was and still IS the sweetest person you'd ever want to know, but, back when he was stuck with that body, nobody got close enough to find out.

40

We tried to get Konigswasser back into his old body to lead us when we first started having the Pioneers' Day Parade, but he wouldn't have anything to do with it, so we always have to flatter some poor boob into taking on the job. Konigswasser marches, all right, but as a six-foot cowboy who can bend beer cans double between his thumb and middle finger.

Conclusion

While there are many other strategies for interpreting works of literature, this chapter has covered three important ones: the role of the narrator, figurative language (including metaphors and symbols) and structure. These three strategies encompass several others, including imagery and allusion, so if you begin by mastering analysis using these three approaches, you will be able to make great strides toward giving a sophisticated reading of any literary work.

Additional resources

- For more insight into the way metre and rhyme work in poetry, try *How to Read Poetry Like a Professor* by Thomas C Foster.

- For a thorough introduction to the concept of the hero's journey and its meaning in literary works, read *Hero With a Thousand Faces*, by Joseph Campbell.

- The authors of this text have also written a text for the DP Literature course, *Literary Analysis for English Literature*. That is a book-length treatment of the topics covered in this chapter, and so it goes into much more depth than is possible here.

Works cited

Austen, Jane, *Persuasion* (Illustrated by Hugh Thomson), 2016, Web, **http://digireads.com/**

Bishop, Elizabeth, 'The Fish', *The Complete Poems: 1927–1979*, New York: Farrar, Straus and Giroux, 1984 (print) (pages 442–44).

Bishop, Elizabeth, 'The Prodigal', *The Complete Poems: 1927–1979*, New York: Farrar, Straus and Giroux, 1984 (print) (page 71).

Booth, Wayne C, *The Rhetoric of Fiction*, Chicago: University of Chicago Press, 2008 (print).

Borges, Jorge Luis, 'Adam Cast Forth', *All Poetry*, Web, accessed 13 December 2018, **https://allpoetry.com/Adam-Cast-Forth**

Browning, Robert, 'My Last Duchess', *Poetry Foundation*, Web, accessed 11 December 2018, **www.poetryfoundation.org/poems/43768/my-last-duchess**

Burns, Robert, 'A Red, Red Rose', *Poetry Foundation*, Web, accessed 12 December 2018, **www.poetryfoundation.org/poems/43812/a-red-red-rose**

Cluck, Nancy Anne, 'Showing or Telling: Narrators in the Drama of Tennessee Williams', *American Literature*, vol. 51, no.1. March 1979, (pages 84–93), Web, accessed 12 December 2018, **https://bit.ly/2HMvl6U.**

'Dolphin Symbolism, Totems and Dreams', Spirit Animal Totems, 13 October 2018, Web, accessed 13 December 2018, **www.spirit-animals.com/dolphin-symbolism/**

Duffy, Carol Ann, 'Demeter', *New Selected Poems 1984–2004*, London: Picador, 2004 (print), (page 200).

Duffy, Carol Ann, 'Ithaca', *Rapture*, New York: Faber and Faber, 2005 (print) (page 50).

Duffy, Carol Ann, 'Valentine', *Selected Poems*, London: Picador, 2015 (print), (page 208).

Fitzgerald, F Scott (1925), *The Great Gatsby*, New York: Scribner, 1995 (print).

Fugard, Athol, '*Master Harold*' … *and the Boys: A Drama*. Media Production Services Unit, Manitoba Education, 2012.

Geary, James, 'In Defense of Puns', *The Paris Review*, 15 November 2018, Web, accessed 13 December 2018, **www.theparisreview.org/blog/2018/11/15/in-defense-of-puns/ ?fbclid=IwAR378kHLgyp_HqnMUjwEsE3d-KvGxs4XEvKJYMMCh4iry-kgckUAn5AVDBQ**

Goodison, Lorna, 'Farewell Wild Woman (I)', *Selected Poems*, Ann Arbor: University of Michigan Press, 1992 (print) (page 115).

Hawley, Noah, *Before the Fall*, New York: Grand Central Publishing, 2017 (print).

Hughes, Langston, *The Collected Poems of Langston Hughes*, Arnold Rampersad, ed., New York: Vintage Books, 1995 (print).

Mansfield, Katherine, 'The Garden Party', *Katherine Mansfield Short Stories*, Katherine Mansfield Society, Web, accessed 15 December 2018, **www.katherinemansfieldsociety.org/ short-stories-by-katherine-mansfield/**

Ng, Celeste, *Little Fires Everywhere*, London: Little, Brown, 2018 (print).

O'Connor, Flannery, 'Everything That Rises Must Converge', New York: Farrar Straus and Giroux, 1965 (print) (pages 3–23).

Poe, Edgar Allan, 'The Tell-Tale Heart', *The Tell-Tale Heart – Poe's Works*, The Poe Museum, Web, accessed 11 December 2018, **www.poemuseum.org/the-tell-tale-heart**

Present Tree, The, 'Every Olive Tree Has A Story …', Web, accessed 13 December 2018, **https://thepresenttree.com/blogs/news/olive-tree-meaning**

Robbins, Tom, 'Lost in translation', *Wild Ducks Flying Backward: The Short Writings of Tom Robbins*, London: Bantam Books, 2006 (print) (pages 209–11).

Rostand, Edmond, *Cyrano De Bergerac*, *The Project Gutenberg EBook of Cyrano De Bergerac*, Project Gutenberg, Web, accessed 11 December 2018, **www.gutenberg.org/files/1254/ 1254-h/1254-h.htm**

Setterfield, Diane, *The Thirteenth Tale*, London: Orion, 2013 (print).

Shakespeare, William, 'Sonnet 73', Academy of American Poets, Web, accessed 12 June 2017, **www.poets.org/poetsorg/poem/time-year-thou-mayst-me-behold-sonnet-73**

Shakespeare, William, *Romeo and Juliet*, Rebecca Niles and Michael Poston, eds., Folger Digital Texts, Folger Shakespeare Library, Web, accessed 18 December 2018, **www.folgerdigitaltexts. org/?chapter=5&play=Rom&loc=p7**

Shakespeare, William, *Taming of the Shrew*, Rebecca Niles and Michael Poston, eds., *Folger Digital Texts*, Folger Shakespeare Library, Web, accessed 18 December 2018, **www. folgerdigitaltexts.org/?chapter=5&play=Shr&loc=p7**

Sharman, Ruth, *Birth of the Owl Butterflies*, London: Picador, 1997 (print).

Swyler, Erika, *The Book of Speculation*, London: Corvus, 2016 (print).

'Turquoise – Meaning & Healing', *Energy Muse*, Web, accessed 13 December 2018, **www. energymuse.com/turquoise-meaning**

Uroff, MD, 'Sylvia Plath and Confessional Poetry: A Reconsideration', *The Iowa Review*, 8.1, 1977, (print) (pages 104–15).

Vonnegut, Kurt, 'Unready to Wear' (*The Galaxy Project*), Barry N Malzberg, ed., New York: Rosetta Books, 2011 (print). Originally published in *Galaxy* magazine in 1953.

Wilder, Thornton, *Our Town: A Play in Three Acts*. London: Harper Perennial Classics, 2003 (print).

Wright, Judith, 'Legend', *PoemHunter.com*, 27 March 2010, Web, accessed 15 December 2018, **www.poemhunter.com/poem/legend-4/**

Approaches to visual texts

One of the assessment objectives of the Language A: Language and Literature course is to: 'analyse and evaluate ways in which the use of language creates meaning'. *Language* includes non-verbal forms of communication, not just verbal. As you have seen in the previous chapters, you will have the opportunity to explore a range of text types throughout your course of study. This includes written or performance-based texts as well as visual texts. Some texts will include both visual and verbal elements, and it is important in these instances that you consider the interplay between text and image.

Reading a visual text is a different experience to reading a literary work or newspaper article or anything else we might consider a more traditional type of text. When you approach a visual text, you can still use content, context, style and structure as the lenses through which to focus your analysis. However, the tools that a visual artist uses to create meaning differ from the traditional linguistic tools that a writer may use. Visual texts require you to develop a new vocabulary. This is why we have devoted a separate chapter to unpacking visual language. We will begin by examining some techniques that are common to most visual texts, whether these be photographs, advertisements or films. We will also look at graphic novels and political cartoons as specific types of visual texts and examine their structural characteristics in more detail.

English Language and Literature is not a media studies course, nor is it an art or film course, so we will not go into as much depth as you would expect to if you were a student of one of these arts. But it is important to have a general understanding of the elements of style that can be found in visual texts so that you can better appreciate how those elements shape meaning. If you are interested in learning more about a specific visual medium, we have recommended some additional resources at the end of the chapter.

Visual techniques

KEY TERMS

Composition – in a visual text, everything that is included or omitted from an image.

Rule of thirds – a compositional technique used in photography whereby the photograph (or image) is divided into thirds, with the dominant part of the image (the subject, or focus) positioned at one of the points of intersection.

An image is composed of many different elements, or stylistic features, much like a poem is composed of literary devices such as rhythm, imagery, metaphor, etc. You will most likely be familiar with many of the stylistic devices discussed in the earlier chapters, but unless you have a background in visual arts, most of the devices presented here will be new to you. This section contains some of the most common visual features you will need to be familiar with when approaching image-based texts, particularly on Paper 1. This list should not be viewed as definitive. Indeed, there are many more technical terms and nuanced techniques relevant to photography, painting, film making and other visual media, but it is not necessary for you to learn all of those techniques to demonstrate an understanding of how language creates meaning.

■ Composition

Composition refers to everything that is included or omitted from an image. Much like the way a poem might be constructed using structural devices such as lines and stanzas, metre and rhyme, an image will be constructed using many of the tools outlined here (angles, colour, contrasts, etc).

■ Rule of thirds

The **rule of thirds** is a compositional technique often associated with photography. The basic premise is that the photograph (or image) should be divided into thirds, with the dominant part of the image (the subject or focus) positioned at one of the points of intersection. This technique is demonstrated in the photograph below.

KEY TERMS

Negative space – the space around a subject. Providing a lot of negative space often gives more focus to a subject.

Salience – when referring to an image, means the dominant part of the image, or that which first attracts the eye's attention.

There is a deliberate use of **negative space** here to draw attention to the subjects riding on a deserted beach at low tide. The dominant expanse of the beach in the foreground, which takes up roughly two-thirds of the image, emphasises the riders' solitude and their placement towards the left and centre of the photograph reflects their forward motion.

■ Salience

The word *salient* means prominent, important or noticeable. **Salience**, when referring to an image, means the dominant part of the image, or that which first attracts the eye's attention. An image can be made salient through a combination of features such as placement, colour or size.

The Brazilian mobile phone company Claro released a series of ads in 2012 to deter people from using their phones whilst driving. In all of the ads, the sailent image is the 'road', which, on closer inspection, is actually a letter. The eye then travels from the bottom of the image to the top, where a series of obstacles are placed. This design reinforces the ad's message of 'Don't text and drive'. View the ads online by reading the QR code given (or type the key search terms 'Claro one letter is all it takes campaign' into a search engine). Our perspective as the audience mimics that of the distracted driver, who only notices the family crossing the road – or the cyclists or the objects in the other images – at the last minute. Their size and position in the background makes them a secondary focus, much like they would be in the real-life situation that the ad is drawing attention to.

■ Camera angle

Photographers and filmmakers use different angles when composing a shot to achieve a specific effect. A certain angle may emphasise part of the image, suggest relationships between subjects, establish tensions or create a dramatic effect. Common angles include bird's eye, bug's eye, long shot, close up and high or low angle.

A ceramic cup photographed using different camera angles, including bird's eye low and high angle and a front angle

■ Perspective

Perspective in art and photography refers to the depth and spatial relationships between objects. Photographers can achieve perspective through a combination of elements such as camera angles, framing, lines, size and positioning. Perspective can be manipulated to create an illusion for a specific effect, as is often seen in advertisements like this one from the perfume brand Dior. The image below left shows a woman looking into her vanity mirror. Her position, along with her reflection, combined with the shape of the mirror and the placement of the perfume bottles, makes the image look like a skull, which is appropriate given that the name of the perfume that is being advertised is *Poison*. This image is itself a **pastiche** of a 19th-century drawing entitled *All Is Vanity* by American illustrator C Allen Gilbert, shown below right.

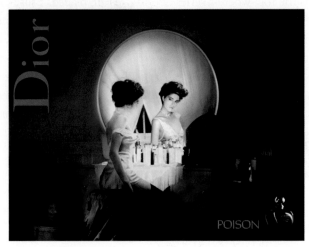
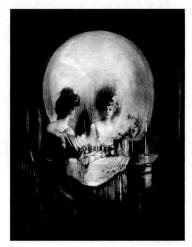

■ Juxtaposition

Juxtaposition is the contrast of two unrelated objects, images or ideas placed next to each other. For example, the British graffiti artist Banksy's *Show Me the Monet* (2005), shown on the next page, juxtaposes the images of shopping carts and a traffic cone with the natural, garden-like surroundings. One possible way of interpreting the effects of this contrast is posed by *The Art Story* in their article 'Important Art by Banksy': 'by representing these man-made objects as discarded in an otherwise beautiful natural setting, he [Banksy] critiques contemporary society's disregard for nature in favor of commodity fetishism and the production of excessive waste'. This image is also an example of allusion or intertextuality; the work is in fact a pastiche of Monet's famous painting *Bridge Over a Pond of Water Lillies* (1899).

Takes one life every 25 seconds*

Drive Safe

The
Frontier Post
www.thefrontierpost.com

* WHO Fact Sheet N 358, March 2013

■ Symbols

As in a literary work, images often contain objects which represent certain ideas. The image on the left, from *The Frontier Post*'s 'Drive Safe' campaign, is a good example of symbolism. The car keys are positioned to resemble a handgun, which represents the idea of violence. By using this symbol, the message is clear: a vehicle can be just as deadly as a weapon.

■ Allusion

Allusions, which are references in a text to other works of literature, art, history or religion are common in literary works and in some non-literary texts such as speeches. Allusions can also be visual, as we see in the example on the left (and in the earlier pastiche of *All Is Vanity*). In this political cartoon by Steve Bell from November 2018 (more on this type of text on pages 78–9), UK Prime Minister Theresa May is being compared to Captain Ahab of *Moby Dick*. Here, May's 'white whale' (or obstacle) is the Brexit deal. Representing this issue visually heightens the impact on the audience, serving as a sort of visual hyperbole.

■ Colour

Finally, and perhaps most importantly, colour is a significant stylistic feature that you should consider when analysing a visual text. Colours can have an emotional impact on us and, depending on the context, can serve a symbolic purpose. Some colours have cultural significance. For example, in most modern Western cultures the colour pink represents femininity and is often associated with girls, while blue is associated with boys. This was not always the case, though, and in some cultures, such as the Far East, blue is seen as the softer, more feminine colour.

Colours can influence our moods and are therefore an effective advertising and marketing tool. Colour theory and psychology is far too complex to cover here in detail, but the article 'The Meaning Of Colour In Marketing' at **https://bit.ly/2UtmBWv** shows that colours generally represent certain universal ideas and are used in specific ways by marketers.

■ Additional film elements

It is unlikely that you will spend much time analysing films in detail in your study of Language and Literature, but it is possible that you might encounter short film clips such as documentaries or advertisements in the context of the language portion of the course. It is worth knowing that many of the techniques outlined in the Visual techniques section which begins on page 69, will apply to film. In addition, you should consider techniques such as camera movements, lighting and sound. Some suggested resources for further reading on film techniques are provided at the end of the chapter. If one of your IB subjects happens to be film, you will likely already have a toolkit at your disposal.

ACTIVITY 1: VERBAL-VISUAL INTERPLAY IN ADVERTISEMENTS

Consider the following Chevrolet advertisement (from 2007). How do the visual and verbal language work together to serve the intended purpose and reach the advert's target audience?

Now that you have examined the advertisement, consider it in comparison to this Chevrolet advertisement from 1947. How might the use of imagery (and text) reflect the respective contexts of composition?

Graphic novels

Some people use the terms *comic book* and *graphic novel* interchangeably, but critics and scholars are in general agreement that the two text types are not the same. A comic book tends to be part of a longer series and is usually structured sequentially around a simple storyline. A graphic novel usually involves a more complex plot structure, often divided into chapters, with deeper themes. Graphic novels include many of the same elements you would find in a traditional novel: characterization, foreshadowing, symbolism, allusions and so on; it's just that a graphic novel takes you on a visual journey through the story rather than leaving everything to your imagination.

There are a number of structural features of graphic novels which you need to be familiar with. Graphic novelists will use these features in different ways to achieve specific effects, as we will see in the examples and activity that follow.

STRUCTURAL FEATURES OF GRAPHIC NOVELS

✔ **Panel**: the box or segment that contains the image and text. A page may be made up of several panels or of a single panel if the graphic novelist's intention is to emphasize the action in that one panel.

✔ **Frame**: the border that surrounds the panel. In some cases, there may be no frame around the panel; if this is the case, the graphic novelist will have had a reason for omitting this feature.

✔ **Gutter**: the space between the panels. The audience is invited to 'read' between the lines of each panel and imagine what may occur in the space between each image (the gutter).

✔ **Bleed**: when an image goes beyond the borders of the page. A bleed may be used to emphasize a particular panel, the absence of a border often serving as a symbol.

✔ **Graphic weight**: the heaviness or intensity of a line or block of shading for visual focus. The bolder the graphic weight, the greater the visual focus, making that element more salient in the scene.

✔ **Caption**: a box or section of text which gives details of the scene in the panel; captions function as narration or voice-over.

✔ **Speech bubble**: a shape (usually a bubble) that contains the dialogue spoken by different characters within a scene.

✔ **Thought bubble**: similar to the speech bubble, this shape (usually that of a cloud) contains the internal monologue of a character.

✔ **Emanata**: lines or graphics which indicate the emotions of the figures or characters on the page.

✔ **Special effects**: the use of onomatopoeia (CRASH! BOOM! for example) or other sound devices to create a dramatic effect on the page.

✔ **Layout**: when we refer to the layout of a graphic novel (or any visual text, for that matter), we are talking about how all of the elements are composed on the page and how those elements work together to create meaning. *Layout* is a general term; when you are analysing a page from a graphic novel, you need to be specific about which aspects of the layout achieve specific effects.

Art Spiegelman's graphic novel *Maus* is arguably one of the most famous examples of the genre – and the first of its kind to win a Pulitzer Prize. Originally published in serial format in the 1980s, the text is more of a graphic *memoir* about Spiegelman's father Vladek's experience as a survivor of the Holocaust. When it was published in novel form, it was subtitled *A Survivor's Tale* and included two parts: *Maus I: My Father Bleeds History* and *Maus II: And Here My Troubles Began*. The novel is narrated by Art, who relates Vladek's story through a frame narrative, and reflects themes such as memory, guilt and survival. Perhaps the most interesting feature of the novel is Spiegelman's choice to depict the Jews as mice and the Nazis as cats, a visual symbol of the power dynamic between the two groups.

Spiegelman uses some of the structural elements of the graphic novel to achieve specific effects. In one particular scene, Vladek and Anja (the parents of the main story's narrator – Art) arrive at Auschwitz. We recommend finding a copy of this graphic novel as it is a useful example in which to find many of the structural features we have listed. This scene is on page 157. There is much to note this scene, so we will focus on a few of the most striking elements. Graphic elements and stylistic devices are highlighted in yellow to draw your attention to the 'language' of the text.

The first panel does not have a border. Instead, the image of the truck seems to drive towards the edge of the page. This visual technique provides a stark contrast (juxtaposition) to what the prisoners are experiencing inside the truck; unlike the panel, which is free from constraints, they are *caged in*. The caption reading 'A few days later, the trucks came. They pushed in maybe 100 of us' allows us to imagine the scale of the transport: we do not see 100 figures; in fact, those figures that we can make out appear to be cats (the Nazis), so this heightens the claustrophobic atmosphere of the scene. The middle two panels focus on the individual characters of Vladek and Anja, the primary narrator's (Art's) mother and father. The framing of the panels emphasizes their individual experience, and the graphic weight of the panels draws attention to their characters; the other figures are darkly shaded to blend into the background. Finally, the frameless image which bleeds across the bottom of the page dominates the scene. Much like the prisoners would have felt overwhelmed by their arrival at Auschwitz, we, as viewers, are confronted with its image; we cannot look away. The iconic *Arbeit Macht Frei* ('Work Makes You Free') sign at the entrance to the camp juxtaposes the *freedom* of the image.

ACTIVITY 2: JUXTAPOSITION IN *PERSEPOLIS*

Another notable graphic novel is *Persepolis* by Marjane Satrapi. Satrapi's text is similar to Spiegelman's in some ways: it, too, is a graphic memoir and consists of two parts (*Persepolis I: The Story of a Childhood* and *Persepolis II: The Story of a Return*). *Persepolis* is also set against the backdrop of conflict and crisis; in this case, the Islamic Revolution in Iran. *Persepolis* is a popular work in translation (from the original French) and features on the English syllabus of many IB schools.

Find a copy of the text and choose a page for this activity. Comment on the juxtaposition of the images in the panels. We have chosen the last page in a chapter entitled 'The Key'. The titular key was purportedly the key to heaven, given as a propaganda tool by the government to young boys to encourage martyrdom. You can review the answer for this page at the end of the book.

ACTIVITY 3: GRAPHIC ELEMENTS IN *THE ARRIVAL*

Shaun Tan's 2006 book *The Arrival* is a *silent* graphic novel. The book uses only visual imagery to tell the story of an anonymous migrant and his experiences moving to a faraway and unfamiliar land. The time and place of the story is deliberately non-descript to emphasize the universal nature of the migrant's experience, but Tan has suggested that it could be set around the turn of the 20th century to coincide with the great waves of migration from Europe to the United States and Australia. Commenting on his style on the Scholastic website, Tan has stated:

> One of the key reasons behind removing all text from the book is to underline this principle – the main character cannot read or understand everything, so neither should the reader. Yet there is an internal logic within all of the details which can be discerned as the story progresses – how things work and so on – and the absence of written narrative seems to invite a closer visual reading, and a much slower one too. (The Arrival Overview)

Find a copy of the book or review some of the images available on Tan's website via the QR code. Choose a spread and answer the following questions: What visual techniques or graphic novel elements does Tan use and to what effect? What mood is evoked through the imagery? As a creative extension, write the text or dialogue that could accompany the visuals. The answer at the back of the book references the spread with the origami bird.

Political cartoons

Political cartoons have been used by artists as a means of critiquing the ills of society for hundreds of years. The medium's roots can be traced back to 19th century England and James Gillray, who is widely considered to be the father of the political cartoon. An example of Gillray's work is presented on page 78. Modern political cartoons can be found in most major newspapers and online media such as Twitter. Political cartoons are context-dependent; they cannot be truly appreciated without an understanding of the historical, political and sometimes cultural or religious contexts in which they were produced.

Cartoonists use a variety of techniques, including some of the visual techniques explored earlier in the chapter. In addition, many political cartoons will contain symbols and visual metaphors, exaggeration (a sort of visual hyperbole), analogies and irony. Cartoonists often rely on dark humour and satire to make a serious point.

One of the earliest examples of the political cartoon is 'The Plumb-pudding in danger – or – State Epicures taking un Petit Souper' by James Gillray, shown below, which dates back to 1805. The British Library describes the cartoon, which is part of its collection, thus:

> 'The Plumb-pudding [sic] in danger' is one of Gillray's most famous satires dealing with the Napoleonic wars in the early 19th century. British Prime Minister William Pitt sits on the left of the picture opposite Napoleon Bonaparte, both of who tear hungrily at the globe in a bid to gain a larger portion. Though the intention of the piece is simple (by lampooning the avaricious pursuit of international dominance by both the French and British governments), Gillray's grotesque portrayal of the characters suddenly brings the cartoon alive. Note particularly the exaggeration of Pitt's skinny physique and Napoleon's beak-like nose: comical devices that would have quickly identified the subjects to his audience by appealing to popular conceptions of the two men. ('"The Plumb-pudding in danger – or – State Epicures taking un Petit Souper" by Gillray').

Steve Bell, a famous modern British cartoonist, paid tribute to Gillray in a pastiche entitled 'The Baked Bean in Danger' (2015), shown below. Bell used a baked bean instead of the plum pudding to represent modern Britain. The plum pudding was considered a luxury; in contrast, the baked bean is a cheap convenience food which, by the time this cartoon had been published, had come to represent 'austerity Britain'. Then-Prime Minister David Cameron and First Minister of Scotland Nicola Sturgeon are shown cutting into the baked bean, no doubt playing on the growing divide between England and Scotland which came to a head during the 2014 Scottish independence referendum. This power dynamic is represented visually in the way that Cameron seems to dwarf Sturgeon.

ACTIVITY 4: SYMBOLS IN POLITICAL CARTOONS

Look at the following political cartoons. What visual elements do you recognize? How are symbols and visual metaphors used to create meaning?

Conclusion

The emphasis in this chapter has been on stylistic devices which are most common across different types of visual texts, with some extra attention paid to specific visual texts like graphic novels and political cartoons. When you are analysing a visual text, it is important not just to describe what it is that you see but to consider how certain features within the image help shape meaning. Just like a conventional written text will contain elements of language which shape meaning, a visual text has its own *language* which is used to communicate with a particular audience and to convey a specific purpose.

Resources for additional study

Visual analysis is a broad skill, so there is not one definitive go-to source of information that we can recommend. However, there are some websites (listed here) which serve as useful collections of types of visual texts, and can supplement the information that we have introduced in this chapter.

- Matrix Education is an online resource which includes a far more comprehensive list of visual techniques in its Visual Techniques and Film Techniques Toolkits, available at **https://bit.ly/2ScjZP1**

- For specific film techniques, The British Film Institute (BFI) is also a useful resource, available at **https://bit.ly/2DFiX6n**

- Websites like *ADWEEK* (available at **https://bit.ly/1jw9iQR**) and *Ads of the World* (available at **https://bit.ly/2qWXe1S**) pull together some of the best examples of advertising. With the latter website, you can sort through ads by date, by medium, by industry, and by country.

- The Library of Congress's website includes a useful Cartoon Analysis Guide and an archive of historical political cartoons, available at **https://bit.ly/1fpVLXq**. The British Library also includes cartoons from the UK in its online collection.

Works cited

'Ad of The Week – The Frontier – TCS Media', *TCS Media*, Web, accessed 22 December 2018, **www.tcsmedia.co.uk/aotw-the-frontier-post/**

Baird, Mike, 'Two equestrian riders, girls on horseback, in low tide reflections on serene Morro Strand State beach'. *Flickr*, Web, accessed 23 December 2018, **www.flickr.com/photos/mikebaird/2985066755**

Bell, Steve, 'Steve Bell on Theresa May's fight to push through her Brexit deal – cartoon', *The Guardian*, 28 November 2018, Web, accessed 29 December 2018, **www.theguardian.com/commentisfree/picture/2018/nov/28/steve-bell-theresa-may-push-brexit-deal-cartoon**

Bell, Steve, 'Steve Bell on David Cameron and Scotland – cartoon', *The Guardian*, 1 June 2015, Web, accessed 13 December 2018, **www.theguardian.com/politics/picture/2015/jun/01/steve-bell-on-david-cameron-and-scotland**

'Claro', Welovead.com, 2018, Web, accessed 23 December 2018, **www.welovead.com/en/works/details/10bDkotx**

Gillray, James, 'The Plumb-pudding in danger – or – State Epicures taking un Petit Souper', *The British Library*, Web, accessed 13 December 2018, **www.bl.uk/collection-items/the-plumb-pudding-in-danger---or---state-epicures-taking-un-petit-souper-by-gillray**

'Important Art by Banksy', *The Art Story*, Web, accessed 22 December 2018, **www.theartstory.org/artist-banksy-artworks.htm**

Satrapi, Marjane, *Persepolis*, New York: Vintage, 2004 (print).

Scool.Scholastic.Com.Au, Web, accessed 13 December 2018, **www.scool.scholastic.com.au/schoolzone/toolkit/assets/pdfs/The_Arrival.pdf**

Spiegelman, Art, *The Complete Maus*, London: Penguin Books, 2003 (print).

Tan, Shaun, *The Arrival*, London: Hodder Children's Books, 2007 (print).

'The Meaning Of Colour In Marketing | Visual.Ly'.Bit.Ly, 2019, **https://bit.ly/2UtmBWv**

5 Writing about texts

Types of writing

You will have to write about literature several times for your IB course assessments. Higher Level (HL) students will have to write an essay of 1 200–1 500 words about one of the works they study. You will develop your own line of inquiry, but you will be recommended to use one of the central concepts in the course as the basis for your choice.

For the exams at the end of the course, you will have to write two papers: Paper 1 on unseen texts, and Paper 2 – a comparison and contrast essay on texts you studied in your course. For Paper 1, you will get two unseen non-literary texts, each with a question which is not compulsory. Students at Standard Level (SL) will choose one of the texts to write about; students at HL will write about both. For Paper 2, you will get four questions of a general nature about literature, and you will choose one to answer. In your answer you will be expected to discuss two of the works you studied in your course. The restriction will be that you may not write about the works you used for your other components (the internal assessment and the HL essay).

For all three of these assignments, you will have to accomplish three things: directly address the question being asked, demonstrate that you have a sophisticated understanding of the work in your analysis and write your ideas in a logical, coherent and clear way. This chapter will provide you with some ways to develop your skills for these requirements.

■ Summary vs analysis

One of the most important things for you to master in order to write about literature is the difference between **summary** and analysis. While you will need to provide a certain amount of summary to provide context for your analysis, it will be the analysis which must be the focus of your work.

A summary is a description of a text which consists of a retelling of the story. In a summary, there is little to no sense of your voice as a critic; you are merely regurgitating an author's ideas.

An analysis, on the other hand, is an investigation into the elements of a literary work. In an analysis, you are performing the role of literary critic and examining aspects of the work in close detail in order to reach a conclusion. An analysis will have to include a carefully chosen and limited summary, along with quotations, to set the context for your analysis, and to support your thesis or line of argument. However, the main focus must be an interpretation of how the aspects of the text you have chosen to write about contribute to the text as a whole.

If you are familiar with Bloom's Taxonomy, you will know that summary sits at the bottom level of the pyramid as *remember*. Analysis involves the higher order thinking skills that are found at the top of the pyramid: *understand, apply, analyse, evaluate* and *create*.

You will not be able to demonstrate beyond a superficial level of understanding if you merely summarize a text. In order to demonstrate *appreciation* for a text you will need to dig deeper and really consider the effects of the tools that the writer has used.

■ Example: Letter from Sullivan Ballou

Read the following letter, written by Sullivan Ballou, Judge Advocate of the Rhode Island militia during the American Civil War, and then examine the responses below. Notice the difference between the summary and the analysis. Consider what characterizes each response.

July 14, 1861

Camp Clark, Washington

My very dear Sarah: The indications are very strong that we shall move in a few days—perhaps tomorrow. Lest I should not be able to write again, I feel impelled
5 to write a few lines that may fall under your eye when I shall be no more …

I have no misgivings about, or lack of confidence in the cause in which I am engaged, and my courage does not halt or falter. I know how strongly American Civilization now leans on the triumph of the Government and how great a debt we owe to those who went before us through the blood and sufferings of the
10 Revolution. And I am willing—perfectly willing—to lay down all my joys in this life, to help maintain this Government, and to pay that debt …

Sarah my love for you is deathless, it seems to bind me with mighty cables that nothing but Omnipotence could break; and yet my love of Country comes over me like a strong wind and bears me unresistibly on with all these chains to the
15 battle field.

The memories of the blissful moments I have spent with you come creeping over me, and I feel most gratified to God and to you that I have enjoyed them for so long. And hard it is for me to give them up and burn to ashes the hopes of future years, when, God willing, we might still have lived and loved together, and seen our sons grown
20 up to honorable manhood, around us. I have, I know, but few and small claims upon Divine Providence, but something whispers to me—perhaps it is the wafted prayer of my little Edgar, that I shall return to my loved ones unharmed. If I do not my dear Sarah, never forget how much I love you, and when my last breath escapes me on the battle field, it will whisper your name. Forgive my many faults and the many
25 pains I have caused you. How thoughtless and foolish I have often times been! How gladly would I wash out with my tears every little spot upon your happiness …

But, O Sarah! If the dead can come back to this earth and flit unseen around those they loved, I shall always be near you; in the gladdest days and in the darkest nights … always, always, and if there be a soft breeze upon your cheek, it shall be my breath,
30 as the cool air fans your throbbing temple, it shall be my spirit passing by. Sarah do not mourn me dead; think I am gone and wait for thee, for we shall meet again …

Summary

Sullivan Ballou wrote this letter to his wife to explain to her why he felt it was so important for him to fight in the Civil War, even though it meant that he had to be away from her and their son. He also wished to convey to her the depth of his love for her, in case he were to be killed in battle.

Analysis

Sullivan Ballou used several stylistic elements in order to achieve his dual purpose of conveying to his wife his deep commitment to his country and his enduring love for her.

The most prominent feature of the letter is its perspective, which is first-person, and which focuses on his own personal feelings. The letter and all the claims in it are authoritative, because the writer speaks for himself.

The tone of the declarations is impassioned – both with regard to his feeling about his duty to his country and with regard to his feelings for his wife. When he talks about his commitment to the Union cause, he says that he is 'willing—perfectly willing to lay down all my joys in this life' for that cause (lines 10–11). The repetition of willing with the intensifier 'perfectly' creates that tone of sincere devotion. When he talks about his feelings for his wife, Ballou uses the image of his joyful memories 'creeping over me'. We understand that he is immersed in those memories as if they are a living thing come to encompass him. We get a clear sense, then, of the depth of his happiness with his wife.

Understanding the context in which the letter was written helps us appreciate the reason for Ballou's writing the letter. He was a soldier in the Union army writing not long after the war started. His regiment was sent to Bull Run for its first engagement, and Ballou was expecting to have to fight in his first battle. The awareness of the possibility of his death has, as he says in lines 4–5, 'impelled' him to write a letter for his wife to read '... when I shall be no more.' The poignancy of that sentence is heightened for the reader who knows that, in fact, Sullivan Ballou was killed in that battle a week later.

Note that the summary is quite a bit shorter than the original (446 words in the extract and 65 words in the summary), but that it includes mention of all the major events/ elements of the passage. This would be too much summary to use in an essay focused on a particular topic relative to the passage. Note also that the analysis, although it is much longer than the summary (313 words), does not include everything that could have been said about what this passage means or what it says. The writer of the analysis had to choose important elements, and so chose to focus on perspective, tone and context. You will never have time to write about everything you notice in a passage or work. The elements that were chosen are those which the writer felt were the most important ones that contribute to Sullivan Ballou's intention in writing to his wife.

Finally, notice the difference between the verbs used in the summary and the verbs used in the analysis. The verbs in the summary are 'fight', 'be away from' and 'be killed'. These are things that the narrator expects might or will happen in his life. This is typical of a summary: when summarizing, you describe what the writer or speaker *does* in his or her life. That is very different from what you do in the analysis. Here are some of the verbs from the analysis: 'used stylistic elements', 'speaks for himself', 'talks about', 'uses the image' and so on. All of these verbs describe what the speaker is doing in terms of shaping his telling of the story. Summary focuses on actions in the dramatic moment; analysis focuses on construction of stories.

■ Dramatic situation vs narrative situation

In any text with a speaker or narrator (that is any text except a drama), the reader must deal with two different situations:

- The dramatic situation – the situation in which the actions of the story occur.

- The narrative situation – the situation in which the narrator tells the story.

Think of the extract in Chapter 3 from 'The Tell-Tale Heart' by Edgar Allen Poe (page 43): that has a first-person narrator, and in that short story, the narrator directly addresses a listener and indicates that he is about to tell a story of past events. We don't know how much time has passed since the events of the story he tells, but we do know that enough time has passed that the narrator, who has committed a crime, has been discovered for it. We presume that he has been examined and determined to be mad, because the narrator's intention of telling the story is to demonstrate that he is not mad.

In the letter on page 83, Sullivan Ballou is writing in the present moment, as his thoughts occur to him. He is not primarily writing about past events, though he refers to some past events in order to portray their significance; he is mainly focusing on future events – things that might happen. Ballou's orientation to his subject is very different from the orientation of the narrator of 'The Tell-Tale Heart' to his subject. In 'The Tell-Tale Heart', the narrative situation takes place some significant amount of time after the events of the dramatic situation, while in the Sullivan Ballou letter, the narrative situation occurs before the imagined events of the dramatic situation. The power of the letter comes, in part, from the fact that present-day readers know that the imagined events did, in fact, come to pass.

Summary is the description of the events of the dramatic situation. Analysis is the reader's observation of how the narrator is telling the story, the identification of the various elements of that story-telling process, and the explanation of how those elements create meaning.

■ Author vs narrator

One decision you will always have to make when writing about texts is whether you are writing about what the *author* does or what the *narrator* or *speaker* does. This decision always poses an interesting problem in a literary work because in a fictional work or a poem, the author creates the narrator or speaker, so it is fair to say that everything the narrator or speaker does is something that the author made him or her do. In a non-fiction, non-literary text, however, the *speaker* or *narrator* is very often the author speaking directly for him or herself.

In making your decision, then, you will need to carefully consider where you want to focus your attention. The box below (Identifying the voice) contains some important considerations.

IDENTIFYING THE VOICE

✔ Is the text a literary work or a non-literary text?

✔ If the text is a non-literary text:

- The writer is probably speaking for him or herself and presenting his or her own ideas, attitudes, values and beliefs in a pretty direct way. You can write about what the author *says*, *believes*, *claims* and so on.
- You do not have to worry about the problem of the speaker or narrator who does not represent the views of the author.

✔ If the text is a literary work, you must first take note of whether the work uses a first-person narrator or speaker, or a third-person one:

- If you have a third-person narrator, it is not particularly interesting to consider what the narrator is doing, because the narrator is not a character in the story, and so his or her actions and attitudes do not influence the story. In that case, focus on what the author is doing to create the effects that you notice.

- If, on the other hand, you have a first-person narrator who is a character in the story, then you have someone whose actions and attitudes do influence the story, and it is definitely important to consider how.
- If, furthermore, you have a reliable first-person narrator (refer back to Chapter 3, page 42, for the difference between a reliable narrator and an unreliable one), then you don't have to worry too much about how the narrator's efforts to tell the story differ from the author's, and you can safely choose to discuss either the author's strategies or the narrator's.
- If, however, you have an unreliable first-person narrator (again, refer back to Chapter 3, page 42), then you definitely need to show that you understand that fact. You will need to demonstrate that you understand what the narrator is up to, how the narrator's strategies effectively misrepresent reality and to what extent. In a full-length essay, eventually you would also want to address the question of *why* the author created such a narrator. You would need to show, in other words, how the author's values, attitudes and understanding of the world differ to those of the narrator.

In the analysis of the Sullivan Ballou letter, the writer did not differentiate between the voice of the piece and the voice of the author. That decision was the correct one for that text because the text is a personal letter, intended to be heard as the author's voice directly.

▩ Assessing the effectiveness of the sample analysis

Now imagine that you were going to write the analysis of the Sullivan Ballou letter shown above. Imagine further that the prompt you were provided in order to help focus your thinking (as for Paper 1) was:

> Choose at least one important stylistic technique from the passage. Identify it and explain its significance.

If we consider the three requirements that we said you need to meet when writing about texts, the sample analysis on page 83 fulfils all three. First, it does directly answer the question as it was asked: the writer chose the stylistic techniques of perspective, tone and context, identified where they can be seen in the passage and then explained that the function of those three techniques was to work together to reveal the quality of Ballou's commitment to his wife and to his country. Second, it is analysis, not summary. It locates significant elements (perspective, tone and context) rather than simply retelling the story. Third, it is well written. Later in this chapter, we will examine some features of clear, strong writing.

▩ Including an appropriate amount of summary

Finally, we considered earlier that you will need to provide a certain amount of summary in order to set the context for your analysis. When you are writing analysis essays, you must presume that you are writing for an educated audience, in this case an audience familiar with reading and analysing texts, but that your reader might not be familiar with this particular work. You must, therefore, provide whatever summary is relevant to the focus of your analysis, so that your reader will understand enough about what is happening to follow your argument – but no more!

Here is a summary that would be appropriate for the Sullivan Ballou letter as an introduction to the analysis provided on page 83:

> Sullivan Ballou, a major in the Civil War, wrote this letter to his wife on the eve of battle so that, in case he was killed, she would know his feelings.

That should be enough for a reader to be able to understand the rest of the analysis. Note how this summary is tailored specifically to what was said in the analysis, and that it is a good bit shorter than the summary in the box (31 words as opposed to 65), which was intended to be a summary of the entire letter.

ACTIVITY 1: WRITING A SUMMARY AND AN ANALYSIS

Read the extract from Ijeoma Oluo's article 'Colin Kaepernick's national anthem protest is fundamentally American' which appeared in the US edition of the London newspaper, *The Guardian*, and write a summary of the whole extract as well as an analytical paragraph. Assume that you have been given the following guiding question: 'What are the two most important stylistic techniques used in the passage to convey the author's meaning?' Although you may choose to ignore this guiding question as you can on your Paper 1, the comments at the end of the book have been written on the assumption that the practice analysis *does* address that question. Finally, write the short summary that you would need to include in order to give context to your analysis.

I was on family vacation when Colin Kaepernick decided to make me care about football. During Friday night's preseason game against Green Bay, the 49ers quarterback did what many black people have been waiting for more of our black football players to do for a long time – he protested. It was a quiet protest, the act of sitting during the national anthem, but it was heard around the world.

5

When interviewed after the game, Kaepernick explained: 'I am not going to stand up to show pride in a flag for a country that oppresses black people and people of color. To me, this is bigger than football and it would be selfish on my part to look the other way. There are bodies in the street and people getting paid leave and getting away with murder.'

In many corners, this didn't go over well, to say the least. Some people burned their Kaepernick jerseys. Many argued that, while Kaepernick may be right to be upset by the thousands of black and brown people killed by police in the US, protesting the flag was not the appropriate way to create change. Others asked why he hates veterans – still others, why he hates America. Yet more people asked why he can't just stick to football. But every argument against Kaepernick's protest is wrong. Every single one.

15

Furthermore, many of them are racist. And the backlash against Kaepernick displays how everyday Americans who would never consider themselves racist can get caught in acts of white supremacy.

For starters, there is nothing more American than protest. It's built into our history and our mythology. I imagine that those who think protesting during the National Anthem is un-American think that the Boston Tea Party was a literal tea party with tiny cakes and monogrammed napkins.

20

Just about every major change in this country to bring America closer to its ideals has been brought about by protest. The women's suffrage movement, the Montgomery bus boycott, labor protests, the Stonewall riots – how much time do you have? If someone can call a group of armed ranchers occupying federal buildings over cattle grazing rules 'patriots' while labeling one man sitting to protest the murder of thousands of American citizens 'un-American', it's time for them to examine their biases and priorities.

25

To those arguing that Kaepernick's protest insults veterans: soldiers did not fight and die for a song or a flag. They fought for many other reasons – American ideals of liberty and equality, access to education, economic opportunities, the draft.

30

35

And many of these veterans are people of color, who sacrificed overseas only to come home to a country whose service meant nothing to the police officers who only saw their black skin and deemed them a threat. Veterans like Kenneth Chamberlain Sr, who was shot and killed by police in 2011 when his medic alert necklace was accidentally triggered. Veterans like Anthony Hill, who was shot and killed by police this year while suffering from what relatives described as a nonviolent mental health crisis due to PTSD from serving in Afghanistan. Veterans like Elliott Williams, who was left paralyzed, naked and crying for help, unable to reach food or water, on a jail cell floor for six days in 2011 until he died from his injuries and

40

dehydration. These men signed up to fight for us, and Kaepernick is fighting for them.

And to those who would argue that Kaepernick hates America when he should, as a rich sports star, have no complaints: this is one of the few lines that manages to be condescending, racist and ignorant all at once.

45

Most black people in America did not choose to be here. Most were brought here against their will and still suffer the socio-economic consequences of being treated for hundreds of years as cattle.

50

Black men in America are 3.5 times more likely than white men to be killed by police, the average white household has 15 times the average net worth of the average black household, one in three black men can expect to see prison in their lifetimes, and the infant mortality rate for black babies is up to three times higher than that of white babies. Despite all this, because Kaepernick happened to win the lottery of talent and circumstance to become a professional athlete, he is supposed to ignore the realities of life for so many others who look like him?

55

And as to why Colin Kaepernick can't just stick to football: 68% of professional football players are black, yet only 16% of head coaches are black – and 0% of owners. So if we *haven't* been discussing race in football, we've been neglecting to do so to the detriment of black players who find that they have little representation in the positions that affect their careers.

60

Furthermore, the thought that there's ever a 'bad time' to discuss racial oppression and police brutality is incredibly privileged and harmful. Black Americans do not get to decide when to encounter racism and police brutality in America. People have been killed while cosplaying with a toy sword, while reaching for a cellphone, while walking up the stairs to their own apartment. A brown friend of mine was pushed and kicked a few weeks ago by an elderly white lady for daring to walk in front of her in a crosswalk.

65

We cannot choose when racism affects us, and it is cruel to insist on choosing when discussions of racism affect you. You can be a professional football player, an accountant, a politician, a teacher – if you are black, you cannot escape the harmful and even deadly effects of racism in America. Colin Kaepernick is black every minute of every day of his life, and his money and his fame will not remove that blackness. Nor will they keep him safe

70

when he's out of uniform.

What Kaepernick has done with his simple protest is brave. He has risked his privilege, his fame and his very career to stand with his fellow black and brown people against the systemic oppression that is literally killing us. This is what team spirit looks like when you look beyond jerseys. This is what American values look like when you stand for all Americans.

Summary	Analysis

Short summary appropriate for analysis

Analysing content rather than stylistic techniques

So far, the examples in this chapter have focused on the kind of analysis of technique that you will be required to present in your exam Paper 1, in which you must write about non-literary texts. For the HL essay, you may choose from any of the works you studied in the course (but which you have not used on any other assessment). This means that you might choose to write about literary works for that assessment. For Paper 2, you must write about two literary works.

When writing about literary works, you will still do the same kind of analysis that you would do for a non-literary text. However, you will focus on the kinds of literary techniques that are covered in Chapter 3 of this book, rather than on the stylistic features that are covered in Chapters 2 and 4.

Writing specifically about poetry

When writing about poetry, the same three obligations will apply: address the prompt as assigned, analyse rather than summarize and write clearly and well. There are, however, a few things to consider, particular to poetry.

▪ Understanding the literal

Although you must not focus on summary to the exclusion or reduction of analysis, you also must not ignore the literal and try to jump straight to the figurative. This is an important instruction for writing about prose or drama as well, however, students are more likely to make this mistake with poetry than with any other literary form. There is a strong temptation to leap straight to abstractions, but the literal must always work in any poem, and you must demonstrate that you understand the poem at both levels.

▪ Example: 'The Girl with the Black Hair' by John Shaw Neilson

Consider the following poem, 'The Girl with the Black Hair', by Australian poet John Shaw Neilson, for instance.

> Her lips were a red peril
>   To set men quivering
> And in her feet there lived the ache
>   And the green lilt of Spring.
>
> 5 'Twas on a night of red blossoms,
>   Oh, she was a wild wine!
> The colour of all the hours
>   Lie in this heart of mine.
>
> I was impelled by the white moon
> 10   And the deep eyes of the Spring,
> And the voices of purple flutes
>   Waltzing and wavering.

> Of all the bloom most delicate
>   Sipping the gold air
> 15 Was a round girl with round arms,
>   The Girl with the Black Hair.
>
> Her breath was the breath of roses,
>   White roses clean and clear,
> Her eyes were blue as the high heavens
> 20   Where God is always near.
>
> Her lips were a red peril
>   To set men quivering
> And in her feet there lived the ache
>   And the green lilt of Spring.

On first reading, we can already see that this poem has something to do with a very attractive woman, but one who is extremely dangerous. The word 'peril', which occurs in both the first and the last stanzas, suggests the danger, and it is tempting to leap to the conclusion that the poem is about a woman who should be avoided.

If you read the poem carefully, with an eye to understanding the literal, you will see that the speaker is describing one night on which he encountered this woman and that it was the moon and the springtime which 'impelled' him towards her (line 9). A literal reading reveals that his heart is complicated and perhaps prone to intoxicating experiences (lines 6–8), and that the girl with the black hair is also much more complicated than simply a creature with lips that were a 'red peril' (lines 1 and 21). She is also compared to clean white roses (line 18) and the blue heavens 'Where God is always near' (line 20). A more careful reading, in other words, reveals that the woman has many good qualities in addition to that touch of danger.

From there, you can go on to analyse the images and symbols that will ultimately suggest purity, godliness and rebirth. The many references to flowers suggest sweetness, springtime and beauty. The colour symbolism suggests both evil (the black hair mentioned in the title and in line 16) and purity and freshness (white, blue and green on lines 18, 19 and 24). The purple and gold (lines 11 and 14) suggest royalty. The reference to the moon might suggest Diana, the goddess of the hunt. So, the poem appears to be about the complexity of the feelings that we experience in that moment of first attraction: a complicated interaction between a joyful anticipation and the slight thrill of danger in the face of the unknown and possibly of the forbidden.

▪ Summary vs analysis in poetry

When you are writing about poetry, you have the same obligation to write analysis rather than summary that you have when writing about prose. Writing an appropriate summary of a poem can pose particular difficulties, however, as we saw in the section above regarding the need to ensure you understand the literal level of poems that you study.

Once you do understand the literal, of course, you still have to choose which bits of summary are relevant to your essay. In the example above, for instance, you would not begin an essay with a whole lengthy recounting of the events at the literal level on a stanza-by-stanza basis. You would have to give only a little context and then, as you develop the analysis, provide any additional summary needed. For this poem, you might begin with a statement such as this:

In 'The Girl with the Black Hair,' the narrator captures the essence of the first moment of attraction to a beautiful, but possibly dangerous, woman.

That would be sufficient to start off the essay. From there, you could write an essay analysing the colour imagery, the reference to heaven, the seasonal symbolism and the contrasts, for instance, to demonstrate a claim about the portrait of the complex feelings of early love.

ACTIVITY 2: 'MAY' BY JOHN SHAW NEILSON

Read this poem, also by John Shaw Neilson, and write a summary of the whole poem as well as an analytical paragraph. Be sure that your summary focuses on the literal level – on what happens in the dramatic level of the poem, as opposed to the narrative level – and that your analysis focuses on the way that the speaker is telling the poem, just as you did for the non-fiction passage above. Finally, write the short summary that you would need to include in order to give context to your analysis. When you have finished, you can read the comments on this activity which are at the end of the book.

> Shyly the silver-hatted mushrooms make
>   Soft entrance through,
> And undelivered lovers, half awake,
>   Hear noises in the dew.
> 5 Yellow in all the earth and in the skies,
>   The world would seem
> Faint as a widow mourning with soft eyes
>   And falling into dream.
> Up the long hill I see the slow plough leave
> 10   Furrows of brown;
> Dim is the day and beautiful: I grieve
>   To see the sun go down.
> But there are suns a many for mine eyes
>   Day after day:
> 15 Delightsome in grave greenery they rise,
>   Red oranges in May.

Summary	Analysis

Summary appropriate for analysis

How do you decide which aspects of the text to focus on?

Regardless of which assessment you are writing for, you will have to decide which very few aspects of a work of literature you will focus on in your essay. You will never have time to focus on everything interesting or important from any work – not even from a very short poem. A choice to give a superficial overview of many different aspects of a text will always be a much weaker option than choosing to examine a few aspects of the text deeply and thoroughly. Depth, in other words, is always going to be more successful than breadth in terms of gaining marks.

◼ Focus on what the question directs you to

The decision regarding what to write about is easiest when the assignment or prompt directs you to focus on certain features. Here is a typical question from a past Language and Literature exam. Students are given a text and asked to:

> Comment on the significance of content, audience, purpose and stylistic features.

As we said from the beginning of the chapter, your most important responsibility is to answer the question being asked. When the questions direct you to specific literary strategies or elements of text, then you absolutely must write about those. This question required students to focus on four specific elements of a non-literary text: content, audience, purpose *and* stylistic features. The 'and' is emphasized here to make the point that if you are given this question, you do not have the option to pick and choose among those four elements: you are required to write about all four. That decision was made for you by the examiners who set the question.

Here is a sample question from the May 2013 International Baccalaureate exam:

> Context – historical, cultural or social – can have an influence on the way literary works are written or received. Discuss with reference to at least two of the works you have studied.

This is the kind of question you might encounter on your Paper 2 task. In this case, your obligation is to analyse the effect on the writer or reader of the historical context in which the writer is writing ('the way literary works are written or received'). It would also be reasonable to analyse the effect of the reader's context on his or her understanding of the text, particularly if that context is quite different from that in which the text was written.

So, this question requires you to consider the effect of time and place on either the reader or the writer (note that the question says 'written *or* received', not *and*). That is not optional. What *is* optional is the choice of which two works you are going to compare and contrast with regard to the effect of the historical context. To do a good job, you will need to choose wisely. It would not be a good idea for this question, for example, to choose two texts which were written in the same time and place or by people who are quite similar in cultural outlook. A good essay will show that you understand the effect of context in a sophisticated way, so contrasting works and approaches would be preferable. Perhaps you could write about how an African American reader might receive a novel such as Colson Whitehead's *The Underground Railroad* in contrast to the way that a white Englishman might receive it, and then contrast that to the way the same two readers might receive a novel such as *Pride and Prejudice*, by Jane Austen, about the British upper classes in the early 19th century. In one case, some readers might have a particularly personal understanding of the work because of their experience living in a culture similar to the one in which the author was writing – and was writing about – while in other cases, the readers might find themselves to be more distanced from the work, and less able to understand it on more than a rational basis, because they do not live in the culture which is the subject of the work. Each work requires knowledge of 19th-century history in the respective country. Readers from other countries may lack sufficient knowledge of that history for full understanding. Your ability to identify those kinds of complexities in your comparison/contrast would mark you as a sophisticated reader.

■ Focus on elements that are important to creating meaning

Some writing tasks, such as the essay that HL students will be required to write, are much broader. You will have to choose the work you wish to write about, which aspect of that work you will discuss, and the elements of the text which are relevant to those choices. In such an instance, then, how will you decide?

First, you will need to ensure that whatever you choose is an aspect of the text that you can connect both to the topic you chose and to the meaning of the work you are writing about.

Knowing that you have to focus on analysis, you also know that you must break down the text into the component parts, as well as connect those parts to meaning. An essay which merely identifies the presence of a number of literary strategies or stylistic elements will not earn high marks. Such an essay only does half the job. Don't, in other words, just point out that a newspaper article contains careful justification of all the facts claimed. You will need to point that fact out, but you will then need to connect that fact to the meaning or effect of the article. For example, careful documentation of facts will function to make the article more believable and, therefore, more persuasive. If you are writing about a literary work, do not just point out that there is a symbol in the first stanza of a poem or in a particular paragraph in a novel. Identify the symbol and then explain how it helps you understand the meaning of the work. In the analysis of 'The Girl with the Black Hair' earlier in this chapter, you saw how the writer identified the presence of colour symbolism, and then went on to connect that fact to the idea that at first sight, a beautiful woman might seem to be both dangerous and beautiful and pure.

That last step is crucial to writing a good essay, whether you are writing about a literary work or a non-literary text. Therefore, if you know that a strategy is present, but you cannot explain what it contributes to the meaning, do not choose that strategy.

■ Show off your skill as a reader

Knowing that you have to choose features of the text which contribute to meaning does not narrow down your choices very much. All the literary elements you can identify from any given work contribute to meaning. One important consideration to help you narrow down the choice is that you want to show yourself to be as sophisticated a reader as you possibly can. Some strategies are more complex than others by their nature, both because they are harder to recognize and because they are harder to explain in a meaningful way. Here are some strategies which, if you can discuss them intelligently, will show you to be a sophisticated reader.

■ Structure in a non-literary text

Given the wide range of text types that you will study in your Language and Literature course, it is not possible to identify all the different kinds of structures that you might encounter. A few different types of structure were named in Chapter 2, starting on page 34. These included: chronological, problem–solution, cause–effect, compare–contrast, sequence, classification–division and description. Many other structures that were not mentioned are possible. Your job as a writer, then, will be first to identify the type of structure. If you are dealing with written text, you can approach the problem of identifying structure by reading each paragraph or section (if the text is an advertisement or diagram, for example) and identify the function of that section in creating the author's point. In the Sullivan Ballou letter earlier in this chapter, for example, you might identify the structure as shown below.

■ Example: Letter from Sullivan Ballou

July 14, 1861

Camp Clark, Washington

My very dear Sarah: The indications are very strong that we shall move in a few days — perhaps tomorrow. Lest I should not be able to write again, I feel impelled
5 to write a few lines that may fall under your eye when I shall be no more …

I have no misgivings about, or lack of confidence in the cause in which I am engaged, and my courage does not halt or falter. I know how strongly American Civilization now leans on the triumph of the Government and how great a debt we owe to those who went before us through the blood and sufferings of the Revolution. And I am
10 willing—perfectly willing—to lay down all my joys in this life, to help maintain this Government, and to pay that debt …

Sarah my love for you is deathless, it seems to bind me with mighty cables that nothing but Omnipotence could break; and yet my love of Country comes over me like a strong wind and bears me unresistibly on with all these chains to the
15 battle field.

The memories of the blissful moments I have spent with you come creeping over me, and I feel most gratified to God and to you that I have enjoyed them for so long. And hard it is for me to give them up and burn to ashes the hopes of future years, when, God willing, we might still have lived and loved together, and seen
20 our sons grown up to honorable manhood, around us. I have, I know, but few and small claims upon Divine Providence, but something whispers to me—perhaps it is the wafted prayer of my little Edgar, that I shall return to my loved ones unharmed. If I do not my dear Sarah, never forget how much I love you, and when my last breath escapes me on the battle field, it will whisper your name. Forgive my many
25 faults and the many pains I have caused you. How thoughtless and foolish I have often times been! How gladly would I wash out with my tears every little spot upon your happiness …

But, O Sarah! If the dead can come back to this earth and flit unseen around those they loved, I shall always be near you; in the gladdest days and in the
30 darkest nights … always, always, and if there be a soft breeze upon your cheek, it shall be my breath, as the cool air fans your throbbing temple, it shall be my spirit passing by. Sarah do not mourn me dead; think I am gone and wait for thee, for we shall meet again …

Providing contextual information to establish reason for writing.

Explaining reasons for risking his life.

Comparing his feelings for his wife to his feelings for his country.

Providing an image that reveals his feelings. Expresses his belief that he will survive the battle and the war. Offers a precautionary testament and asks for forgiveness, should it be needed in case of his death.

Imagines a future and assures his wife of his eternal devotion, even after death.

Notice that all the descriptions of the different sections begin with a verb that describes what the speaker (or in this case writer) is doing as a rhetorical action – as a means of making his point. From looking at the descriptions of the sections, we can now describe the overall approach to structure in this letter: Sullivan Ballou moved from the rational to the emotional. He began by taking the very pragmatic steps of explaining himself and his thinking. From there, he moved on to connecting his feelings for his wife, Sarah, to his feelings for his country as a means of revealing his dilemma and showing why he has chosen to go to war and risk his life, despite his love for her. In the final section of the letter – which constitutes the two longest paragraphs and more than half the letter – Ballou shifts to an emotional appeal in which he conveys to his wife the depth of his love for her, his hope that he will return to her and his avowal of everlasting love. In essence, then, he acknowledges the danger of his chosen pursuit, assures Sarah that his choice to accept the danger is not a signal that he does not care about her, and then, in acknowledging the possibility of his not returning, offers her as much comfort as he can. Note that the ability to make a generalized statement about the structure – 'Ballou moved from the rational to the emotional' – reveals an ability to synthesize, which is a more sophisticated ability than the ability simply to note the presence of different sections. You should aim to produce that synthesis.

ACTIVITY 3: ANALYSING STRUCTURE IN AN INFOGRAPHIC

In July 2018, a young Thai soccer team became trapped in a cave in Northern Thailand and were rescued by an international diving team. The incident received much global news coverage and many different infographics were created to show how the soccer players were rescued. Click on the QR code to see an article from Insider describing the rescue mission, including their own infographic of the diving procedure. Examine the infographic titled 'How divers helped the Thai soccer team out' carefully and identify the various elements that contribute to meaning. Make a list of those elements, each with a title which identifies its function. You may wish to consider colours and shapes as well as text. When you have your list, write a two- to three-sentence generalization describing the use of structure in the infographic. There are notes about the infographic at the end of the book for you to review once you have done the activity.

■ Structure in a literary text

It is quite easy to identify formal structures in poems, such as those that you learned about in Chapter 2; however, analysing the function of those structures is much more difficult. Identifying important structural elements in poems that do not have a recognized poetic structure, or in many other kinds of texts such as novels, opinion columns, tweets and diagrams is much harder. Refer to Chapter 3 (page 57) for a review of how to identify structure in prose fiction.

Discovering the structure of a poem which has no formal, named, structural elements is similar to the problem of discovering the structure of a work of prose. You have to consider how the poet or the narrator has constructed the poem in terms of a developing story, a developing argument, or the creation of another type of effect.

The following poem, by Distinguished Professor of English at the University of New Orleans, Nigerian-born Niyi Osundare, has a very interesting structure.

■ Example: 'Hole in the Sky' by Niyi Osundare

(Choreo-poem. Preferably with musical accompaniment, the tempo varying according to the mood and meaning of each section)

Eco-Snaps

i

Koko gbakokodi
Koko didikokodi*

'Tell my story,'
Said the Earth to me,
5   'Oh, tell my story the way it is.
Don't sugarcoat its bile
Don't varnish its rust
Don't cover its scars with pretty words
Tell my pain the way it is
10   The way it is
          The way the way the way it is
Tell my pain,   the way it is.'

Koko gbakokodi
Koko didikokodi

ii

15   The day the river caught fire
And the lake burnt like Devil's oil

The mountain coughed like a broken giant
The sky's eyes were red with grief …

Plants whose lethal spills provoked the plague
20   Lay fortressed behind the hills
Ayekooto** sighted their owners
On their way to the city bank

   Koko gba kokodi

iii

Ever heard fruits arguing between the leaves
25   Over which got the deepest dose
Of the pesticidal plague?

The poison killed the pest
And later buried the people

   Koko gba kokodi

iv

30 The thunder of the sea
Rattles the silence of the sky
Wailing whales wonder about their woes
The deeper the dolphin dives
The shallower its desired relief

35 *Koko gba kokodi*

v

The desert marches towards the sea
The desert marches towards the sea

Fire in its eyes
Mayhem in every movement

40 The desert marches towards the sea

With camel-loads of broken skulls,
Roasting *iroko**** trees for lunch
The mahogany for early dinner.
Dandelions roar beneath its feet.
45 The elephant grass has lost its tusks
To the famished poacher from sandy regions

The desert marches towards the sea
Alas, the boundless rainforest of my youth
Has shrunk to a frightened eyebrow
50 On the forehead of the coast

Koko gba kokodi

vi

The midday sun
Cannot see its face in the lake
The turquoise sea is yellow
55 From the poison of upland plants
The day they killed a tree
In the ancient forest
The chainsaw left a dirge
On the lips of the leaves

60 There is a bird in my heart
Craving for a perch on the absent tree.

Koko gba kokodi

vii

Seasons of omen:
One-legged frogs

65 Babies with missing arms
The grass's green laughter
Has yellowed into sickening groan
Vengeful droughts digest the fields

    Koko gba kokodi

viii
70 A hole
A hole
A blazing hole
In the garment of the sky

Oven-hot summers
75 Winters blind with ice

The Arctic melts like butter
As rising oceans consume the land

Fog-fraught cities grope
Beneath their fuming factories
80 The rain falls, acid,
On frightened forests

The Earth we used to know
Is once upon a time

A hole
85 A hole
A blazing, blinding hole
In the garment of the sky

    Koko gba kokodi

ix
Trumpet sounds in the horizon
90 Green intimations unfurl the wind
Healing needle to the hole in the sky
Earth's Redemption Army
Is gathering strength beyond the clouds.

Trumpet sounds behind the mountains
95 Green intimations unfurl the wind.
    Koko   gba   kokodi

    Koko   didi   kokodi

* Sound of the deep-timbred drum associated with Earthdance.
** Literally: The-world-abhors-the-truth. Yoruba name for parrot, 'radio of the forest'.
*** Highly prized tree in the Nigerian rainforest; famous for its majestic height and durability.

We notice right away that the poet has divided the poem into numbered sections, so, although there is no recognizable standardized poetic form, we can use the guidance of the section numbers to help us figure out what the poet is doing. We also see that there is a repeated refrain at the end of every section, but that the layout of the refrain changes in some sections. The footnote tells us that the refrain is intended to mimic the sound of a drum associated with Earthdance, so we can understand that at the end of each section, we hear the drum beat. A quick overview also reveals that the eighth section is the longest one, so we might expect that section to be particularly important, structurally speaking.

If we go through the poem and describe the nine sections with names, as we did with the Sullivan Ballou letter (page 93) and the infographic (page 94), we might come up with these titles:

i	Earth speaks, asking that her story be told honestly.
ii	Factories poison the Earth, making the owners rich.
iii	Fruits are poisoned, and then the people who eat them.
iv	The creatures of the sea suffer from the poison.
v	The effects of the poison spread, killing off plants and animals and turning more and more of the Earth into desert.
vi	Waters are poisoned and change colour. The ancient trees are killed.
vii	Baby animals and humans are born deformed. Drought kills crops.
viii	A hole in the sky – a hole in the ozone layer – causes acid rain and global warming.
ix	A little sign of hope that the problems can be solved and the Earth restored.

Notice that the elements in each section are not ordered chronologically, but they do give the impression of the effects of the damaging poisons spreading out over the Earth, as more and more parts of the Earth are affected. We could describe the overall structure, then, as follows. The speaker moves from the destruction of the Earth at the beginning of the story, through to a series of effects of the destruction caused by man and his factories, and then ends with the idea that there is hope that the problems can be solved.

Notice, though, that there is not one single correct answer. This is one possible analysis of structure, but you could make an argument for a different structure. The critical requirement is for you to justify the claims you make about how the text is structured – and, ultimately, how that structure contributes to meaning.

■ Symbols

The analysis of symbols is a more sophisticated skill than the analysis of metaphors and similes because symbols are less fixed in meaning and require more imaginative and rational work on the part of the reader. Generally speaking, the comparison is stated in the text for both metaphors and similes, but that overt comparison is often not present for symbols. This 2013 Cheerios commercial, for example, caused a furore in some quarters because it features a mixed-race family. You can access it at **https://bit.ly/1Hqiccd**.

People who were angry were responding to the idea that the inter-racial couple represents – symbolizes – a change in the traditional idea of family. Those who championed the ad were responding to the same thing, only they felt that the traditional idea of a family should be expanded to include more than just couples made up of two people of the same race and white couples. The symbol of the family in this case was powerful enough to cause a huge media backlash, after which General Mills (the maker of Cheerios) temporarily withdrew the ad because the comments on the website were not family friendly (Demby). It was re-released, however, in January 2014. If you were writing about this advertisement, your ability to discuss the role of the symbol of the family in the advertisement would mark you as a sophisticated reader of this visual text. General Mills was deliberately using that symbol (which, because of the medium of the television advertisement, is also a powerful image) to expand their appeal to a potential customer base they had not previously targeted. You would also have to discuss the context in which the advertisement was made (21st century America, which is polarized about racial issues) in order to properly interpret the bold stance that General Mills took in making the advertisement. To appreciate the effect of the symbol, then, you need more sophistication as a reader than you would for less complex metaphors or similes.

When writing about symbols, metaphors or similes, make sure that you identify both parts of the figure. For metaphors and similes, the two parts have names: tenor and vehicle. The vehicle is the object to which the main thing is being compared, while the tenor is the thing that the writer wants the audience to see in a new way. Your job is to figure out which characteristics of the vehicle enlighten us about the nature of the tenor. When Shakespeare has Romeo say:

> But soft, what light through yonder window breaks? / It is the East, and Juliet is the sun. (*Romeo and Juliet*, Act 2 Scene 2, lines 2–3)

Juliet is the tenor and the sun is the vehicle. To interpret the metaphor effectively, we must consider which features of the sun apply to Juliet. We might consider that to Romeo, the relevant features are the fact that the sun is bright, it brings happiness and a sense of well-being, and, as he mentions, it rises in the east bringing a new day. Juliet is, for Romeo, the joy of a new day. Conversely, we might also consider that the sun is a source of life, an enormous ball of fire, and if we were to get too close to the sun, it would burn us to death. Having read the play, we know that that is what happens to Romeo following his relationship with Juliet, so we can see that Shakespeare was foreshadowing something that Romeo couldn't yet know.

We do not use the terminology of tenor and vehicle with symbols; however, the concept is the same. You must consider what the symbol is, and which characteristics of that thing shed light on the object or idea for which it stands.

■ Narrative perspective

KEY TERM

Narrative perspective – the way a story is being told and from whose point of view.

You can review Chapter 3 for the discussion of understanding the **narrative perspective** in prose. The speaker of the poem is not usually called a narrator, because the speaker of a poem is not always narrating an actual story, but all the same important concepts regarding narrators apply to speakers. Speakers of poems can be reliable or unreliable, they can be characters in the dramatic situation or observers, and so on. Narrators in a non-literary text, however, are generally not going to be unreliable – though unintentional unreliability is possible in cases in which the author of the piece is mistaken or even deluded about his or her subject. Consider, for example, the opinion piece 'Should any vaccines be required for childen?' on page 99. This is from the website ProCon.org, which offers opposing viewpoints on controversial subjects with the tagline 'Understand the Issues. Understand Each Other'. The following text is one of a number of arguments on the website supporting the claim that people should not vaccinate their children.

■ Example: 'Should any vaccines be required for children?' – ProCon.org

Vaccines contain harmful ingredients. Some physicians believe thimerosal, an organic mercury compound found in trace amounts in one flu vaccine for children and other vaccines for adults, is linked to autism. [84] Aluminum is used in some vaccines and excess aluminum in human bodies can cause neurological harm.
5 [85] Formaldehyde, also found in some vaccines, is a carcinogen, and, according to VaxTruth.org, exposure can cause side effects such as cardiac impairment, central nervous system depression, 'changes in higher cognitive functions,' coma, convulsions, and death. [86] Glutaraldehyde, a compound used to disinfect medical and dental equipment, is used in some DTaP vaccinations and exposure
10 can cause asthma and other respiratory issues. [86] Some flu vaccines contain cetyltrimethylammonium bromide (CTMB), a compound used as an antiseptic, which can be a skin, eye, and respiratory irritant. Some polio, TD, and DTaP vaccines contain 2-phenoxyethanol, an antibacterial that is a skin and eye irritant that can cause headache, shock, convulsions, kidney damage, cardiac and kidney failure,
15 and death. [86] Some vaccines for the flu contain chicken egg protein, which can be harmful to children who are allergic to eggs. [87] Some vaccines for PCV, HPV, DTaP, Hep A, Hep B, and Hib contain yeast proteins which, according to VaxTruth and Joseph Mercola, MD, an alternative medicine proponent, contain MSG that can cause migraines, irritable bowel syndrome (IBS), asthma, diabetes, Alzheimer's, Lou
20 Gehrig's disease, ADD, seizure, and stroke. [86] [88]

The text includes source citations for many of the claims, so the narrative perspective would appear, on the surface, to be quite reliable. If you investigate closely, however, you will find that the source cited for the first, and possibly most common argument against vaccinating children (that autism is linked to vaccines) is a disreputable one (Snyder). We won't go through all the sources here, but given the fact that the original claim, in a 1998 study, that there is a link between vaccines and autism, was debunked many years ago and the doctor who published it, Andrew Wakefield, has been found guilty of ethical violations (Rao and Andrade), we can see that this writer has based the first point of his or her article on a source that is not credible. Once we know that the writer has misjudged the reliability of one source, we know that his or her own judgement is in question, and so we have a piece with an unreliable narrator. Certainly, we have no cause to think that this writer doesn't believe what he or she has written, but the information in the piece is factually inaccurate; thus, the narrator is mistaken about the story he or she thinks is being told.

If you can identify the narrative perspective of a text and explain how that perspective influences the meaning, you are working at a very sophisticated level of textual interpretation.

IDENTIFYING NARRATIVE PERSPECTIVE

To make a basic interpretation of the narrative perspective, ask yourself these questions:

✔ Who is the speaker or narrator? What can you tell about them as a person? If there is a third person narrator or speaker, you cannot answer this question.

✔ When is the speaker or narrator talking, relative to the events of the dramatic situation? Is it immediately afterwards? Years later? Before the events are even finished?

✔ How is the speaker or narrator speaking? Is there any indication of their emotional state or circumstance that might interfere with their objectivity?

✔ What is the speaker or narrator's relationship to the events about which they are speaking? Do they directly affect him or her?

When writing about the narrative perspective, you would not list these questions and answers. Instead, you would synthesize your answers into a statement describing the narrative perspective.

■ Example: *The Songlines* by Bruce Chatwin

Here is an example of a narrative perspective analysis of the opening passage of Bruce Chatwin's *The Songlines*, a travel book about the Australian bush.

In Alice Springs – a grid of scorching streets where men in long white socks were forever getting in and out of Land Cruisers – I met a Russian who was mapping the sacred sites of the aboriginals.

His name was Arkady Volchok. He was an Australian citizen. He was thirty-three
5 years old.

His father, Ivan Volchok, was a Cossack from a village near Rostock-on-Don, who, in 1942, was arrested and sent with a trainload of other *Ostarbeiter* to work in a German factory. One night, somewhere in the Ukraine, he jumped from the cattle-car into a field of sunflowers. Soldiers in grey uniforms hunted him up and
10 down the long lines of sunflowers, but he gave them the slip. Somewhere else, lost between murdering armies, he met a girl from Kiev and married her. Together they drifted to a forgetful Adelaide suburb where he rigged up a Vodka still and fathered three sturdy sons.

The youngest of these was Arkady.

15 Nothing in Arkady's temperament predisposed him to live in the hugger-mugger of Anglo-Saxon suburbia or take a conventional job. He had a flattish face and a gentle smile, and he moved through the bright Australian spaces with the ease of his footloose forbears.

His hair was thick and straight, the colour of straw. His lips had cracked in the heat.
20 He did not have the drawn-in lips of so many white Australians in the Outback; nor did he swallow his words. He rolled his r's in a very Russian way. Only when you came up close did you realise how big his bones were.

Question	Answer
Who is the narrator?	The narrator is the author, writing about his own personal experience from a trip to the Australian Outback.
When is the narrator speaking?	The author is writing sometime after the end of the trip; we cannot, from this passage, tell how much time has passed between the experience and the telling.
How is the narrator speaking?	The narrator is quite calm and reflective. He is remembering the past without any extreme emotion. He supplies a number of details about the man he met, which suggests that he (the narrator/writer) is an observant person.
What is the narrator's relationship to the events about which he is speaking?	He is speaking of events in which he was directly involved. The story is evidently memoir.
Description of narrative perspective:	The narrative perspective of this passage from 'The Songlines' is a traveller who has had an interesting experience during a trip to Australia and is writing to describe that experience. He appears to be reliable.

Being able to show your understanding of how the narrative perspective and the reliability of the narrator contributes to the meaning of the text is a sophisticated skill, and these questions are a useful prompt to understanding what kind of narrator or speaker you are reading. When deciding whether to write about the narrator, you will have to determine the degree to which that perspective influences our ability to determine the truth about events. Unreliable narrators or speakers are generally more important as literary tools than reliable narrators. Very often, their stories or poems are about those narrators as flawed human beings as much as they are about whatever content those narrators think they are delivering.

ACTIVITY 4: ANALYSING NARRATIVE PERSPECTIVE

Read this speech by King George VI, which dates from 3 September 1939, and answer the questions about the narrative perspective. At the end, write a statement describing the narrative perspective of the speech. Be sure to include a statement as to whether the narrator is reliable. When you have finished, you can read the activity notes at the end of the book.

> In this grave hour, perhaps the most fateful in our history, I send to every household of my peoples, both at home and overseas, this message, spoken with the same depths of feeling for each one of you as if I were able to cross your threshold and speak to you myself.
>
> 5 For the second time in the lives of most of us, we are at war. Over and over again, we have tried to find a peaceful way out of the differences between ourselves and those who are now our enemies; but it has been in vain.
>
> We have been forced into a conflict, for we are called, with our allies,
> 10 to meet the challenge of a principle which, if it were to prevail, would be fatal to any civilised order in the world.

15
It is a principle which permits a State, in the selfish pursuit of power, to disregard its treaties and its solemn pledges, which sanctions the use of force, or threat of force, against the sovereignty and independence of other States.

Such a principle, stripped of all disguise, is surely the mere primitive doctrine that might is right. And if this principle were established throughout the world, the freedom of our own country and of the whole British Commonwealth of Nations would be in danger.

20
But far more than this, the peoples of the world would be kept in the bondage of fear, and all hopes of settled peace and of security, of justice and liberty, among nations, would be ended.

This is the ultimate issue which confronts us. For the sake of all that we ourselves hold dear, and of the world order and peace, it is

25
unthinkable that we should refuse to meet the challenge.

It is to this high purpose that I now call my people at home and my peoples across the seas who will make our cause their own.

I ask them to stand calm and firm and united in this time of trial.

The task will be hard. There may be dark days ahead and war can no

30
longer be confined to the battlefield, but we can only do the right as we see the right, and reverently commit our cause to God. If one and all we keep resolutely faithful to it, ready for whatever service or sacrifice it may demand, then with God's help, we shall prevail.

May He bless and keep us all.

Questions

1 Who is the speaker? What can you tell about the speaker as a person?
2 When is the speaker talking relative to the events of the dramatic situation? Is it immediately afterwards? Years later? Before the events are even finished?
3 How is the speaker speaking? Is there any indication of his emotional state or circumstance that might interfere with his objectivity?
4 What is the speaker's relationship to the events about which he is speaking? Do they directly affect him?

Statement of narrative perspective

■ An important consideration

There is one big caveat, however, to the idea that you ought, if you can, to use one of these more sophisticated literary elements: if there is a 'less sophisticated' literary strategy in a particular work that is absolutely central to the meaning of the work, then you undoubtedly must write about it.

Shakespeare, in his Sonnet 130 ('My mistress' eyes are nothing like the sun'), for instance, uses the simile in the opening line to begin a series of comparisons which ultimately prove to be ironic. If you were to write about that poem and not discuss how the similes and metaphors work, you would fail to demonstrate that you have a good understanding of that poem. Part of your decision-making process then, when deciding what to write about, must be the determination of which literary strategies play the most important role in that particular work.

Finally, diction is generally not a very good choice – at least not if you cannot focus the concept further. 'Diction' just means word choice, and all the words of any text have been chosen. If you can, you should characterize the diction in some way. In almost every case, you can take the word or words you were tempted to call diction and re-categorize them as something else. Many words in English are already metaphors – think of the verb 'fall' used to describe someone losing status or as a noun, as in the biblical 'fall from grace'. Another example is the adjective 'crowning', as in a 'crowning achievement'. In neither case is the action literal; no one physically falls and no one is literally crowned. Because English is so richly riddled with metaphor, you can often discuss the metaphorical use of language instead of simple diction.

If you can label a category such as 'technical jargon', 'financial terminology' or 'religious references', you will be showing a more refined understanding of the choice of words, and you will make it easier for yourself to be able to analyse the function of those words in creating meaning.

Final notes about choice

Your choice of what to write about depends on three important factors that you must take into consideration:

- The specific task assigned.

- The most important elements which contribute to meaning.

- Your ability to show off your skills as a reader.

These three factors are listed in the order of their importance. All three are important, however, so you cannot approach the task of writing about literature with the idea that if you choose the most important one you will have a good essay. You must do all three.

Organization

Once you know what to write about, you are left with the problem of how to organize your essay. You have two aspects of organization to deal with: the organization of the essay as a whole and the organization of each body paragraph, which is where the actual analysis appears.

You are probably used to organizing an essay by writing an introduction with a thesis statement, followed by the body of the essay and finishing with the conclusion. Each of those sections requires a particular set of skills, outlined here.

Introduction

You have probably often heard that the introduction should grab the reader's attention. That might be true, but that is not the sole function of an introduction. An introduction must set up the argument that follows, so it has to be integrally related to the rest of the essay. Something that grabs the reader's attention but does not contribute in a significant way to the argument is a waste of words.

The following pages contain six examples of introductory paragraphs for literary analysis essays. All six are written for the same thesis statement describing an interpretation of EB White's essay, 'Once More to the Lake'. As you read the introductions, consider these points:

- In no case do these paragraphs make statements of anything that the reader is likely to already know.

- The sixth example, 'Ask a rhetorical question', is included only because it is a technique that writers have often been taught and is included here as a warning of what *not* to do!

- These first five types of introductions are useful devices. In writing an effective essay, the writer has the responsibility of selecting whatever type of introduction will most effectively create the intended effect – even if that means writing an introduction which is not one of these types.

- Confident writers will be able to use these techniques in innovative ways, combine them or ignore them altogether.

- There is no rule for writing good introductory paragraphs. Good writing is any writing that gets the job done.

- The job is to mean what you say and say what you mean.

Although these examples are based on a literary work, the same types of introductions can certainly be used for analysis essay about non-literary texts.

■ Type 1: Use a quotation

I walked beside the evening sea
And dreamed a dream that could not be;
The waves that plunged along the shore
Said only: 'Dreamer, dream no more!'
In these lines from 'Ebb and Flow', George William Curtis compares the relentlessness of the sea wearing away at the shore with the hopelessness of trying to hold on to an unattainable dream. EB White takes on the same subject in his essay 'Once More to the Lake', in which he examines the question of whether time has, like Curtis' ocean, the power to erode a person's capacity to dream. In his essay, White tells the story of his experience returning as an adult with his son, to the place where his family vacationed every summer, and, in seeing his son walking in his footsteps, he realizes that he is no longer the young man that he was. The essay explores the question of the dream of our memories of our childhood and shows how losing the vision one has of oneself as a sort of perpetual child means facing the devastating fact of one's own mortality.

Note that this sample combines the use of a quotation with conveying an idea that is in accordance with the ensuing argument of the thesis. A quotation can be used just as effectively when it is setting up an argument only to knock it down (see example Type 4 on page 105).

■ Type 2: Begin with an anecdote

In 'Pride and Prejudice', Jane Austen created a protagonist in Elizabeth Bennet who is a self-assured young woman, and who has long been accustomed to believing in her own intelligence and good judgement. She receives a rather serious shock halfway through the novel when she reads a letter from Mr Darcy which reveals to her that in her judgement of him and of Mr Wickham, she, Elizabeth, has been foolish, ignorant and self-delusional. Memorably, she cries out, after she reads the letter, 'until this moment, I never knew myself'. Elizabeth experiences a moment in which she must surrender her past view of herself and create a new one. In his essay, 'Once More to the Lake', White tells the story of his experience returning, as an adult with his son, to the place where his family vacationed every summer, and, in seeing his son walking in his footsteps, realizes that he is no longer the young man that he was. The essay explores the question of the dream of our memories of our childhood and shows how losing the vision one has of oneself as a sort of perpetual child means facing the devastating fact of one's own mortality.

KEY TERM

Anecdote – an interesting or humorous story about a real-life event.

Note that this example uses a literary anecdote. The anecdote can come from history, personal experience, literature or even current events. Any story that illustrates the idea to come in the thesis, and, subsequently, in the essay, will work.

■ Type 3: Give pertinent background information

In his essay, 'Once More to the Lake', White tells the story of his experience returning to the Belgrade Lake in Maine, where his family vacationed every summer. White first wrote about the lake in a pamphlet when he was 15 (Nordquist). In 1936, White returned to the lake and wrote about it again in a letter to his brother (Nordquist). In 1941, White returned one more time, this time with his own son, and, in seeing his son walking in his footsteps, he realizes that he is no longer the young man that he was. The essay he wrote for 'Harper's Magazine' following that experience explores the question of the dream of our memories of our childhood and shows how losing the vision one has of oneself as a sort of perpetual child means facing the devastating fact of one's own mortality.

Note: The trick here is to provide background information that is necessary (or at least helpful!) for understanding the argument about to come, but that is not intuitively obvious to the most casual of readers. Remember that your audience for an analysis essay is the unknown educated reader, but not one who knows the work or its context in detail.

■ Type 4: Set up a counter argument

We tend to idealize childhood. People often look back on their own childhood through a lens of nostalgia, which casts those years in a sort of perpetually blissful summer. We also find it easy to think of ourselves as being essentially the same person as our childhood selves, so that we become in a way as immortal as our memory of that perpetual summer. In his essay, 'Once More to the Lake', however, EB White shows us that that nostalgic view is not real, and that the recognition of the fact that we are no longer children can be a shocking experience. White tells the story of returning, as an adult with his son, to the place where his family vacationed every summer, and, in seeing his son walking in his footsteps, he realizes that he is no longer the young man that he was. The essay explores the question of the dream of our memories of our childhood and shows how losing the vision one has of oneself as a sort of perpetual child means facing the devastating fact of one's own mortality.

Note that with this type of introduction, the balance of the essay deals with proving the thesis, and the initial argument presented in the introduction is generally not alluded to again – certainly not in any detail.

■ Type 5: Begin with a generality and move to the specific

The mental experience of ageing can be quite deceptive. As we grow older, we tend not to notice that we are changing in any significant way, and we feel the same as we were many years ago. That particular form of mild self-delusion can, however, set us up to have to deal with a shock when we come to face the truth. In his essay, 'Once More to the Lake', EB White tells the story of returning, as an adult with his son, to the place where his family vacationed every summer, and, in seeing his son walking in his footsteps, he realizes that he is no longer the young man that he was. The essay explores the question of the dream of our memories of our childhood and shows how losing the vision one has of oneself as a sort of perpetual child means facing the devastating fact of one's own mortality.

Note that the generality posed should be thought-provoking. Do not make generalities that are statements of the obvious: 'Throughout history, poets have written about love' may be a generality, but it is an insult to the reader's intelligence! The example above is marginally acceptable, but really it is quite difficult to come up with a generality that is both general and subtle!

■ Type 6: Ask a rhetorical question

What does it mean to have to face one's own mortality? In his essay, 'Once More to the Lake', EB White tells the story of returning, as an adult with his son, to the place where his family vacationed every summer, and, in seeing his son walking in his footsteps, he realizes that he is no longer the young man that he was. The essay explores the question of the dream of our memories of our childhood and shows how losing the vision one has of oneself as a sort of perpetual child means facing the devastating fact of one's own mortality.

Type 6 is a popular, but ultimately ineffective, method of writing an introduction. If you read the sample paragraph above carefully, you will see that the rhetorical question first and foremost adds nothing to the paragraph. The author could just as easily begin with the second sentence. The rhetorical question, furthermore, is very difficult to manage in print. The reason a question is rhetorical is that there is presumably only one possible answer to it. So there are three problems:

1   If there is only one possible answer, then the question really is not providing necessary information that the reader doesn't already know.

2   There really are very few questions for which there is only one possible answer (in the example above, for instance, which is typical of what inexperienced writers try with rhetorical questions, there are many possible answers).

3   When there really isn't only one possible answer, the effect on the reader is that, by the nature of the medium, the reader must take in the question as if it were a direct question asked to him or her as an individual. That gives the reader the chance to answer the question for him or herself. and if the answer the reader provides doesn't match the answer the author had in mind, the reader is already thinking something in opposition to your ideas right from the very beginning.

There is, therefore, really only one way to use a rhetorical question effectively, and it is extremely hard to achieve: a rhetorical question works in an argument essay when it has been so masterfully set up that there truly is only one possible answer to the question *given the context in which it is posed*, and that it sneaks up on the reader so that the answer, although the only possible answer in the context, comes as a surprise to the reader. The effective rhetorical question makes the reader do the work of drawing the only possible conclusion, and makes him or her do it right on the spot, so that the idea that the question forces on the reader is new. If you can achieve that, then by all means, use a rhetorical question in your essay. If you cannot, then avoid it. Rather than functioning as a 'eureka' moment, that rhetorical question will function as a signpost to the reader that you are an inexperienced writer using a trick that you have been shown which you don't really understand.

Generally, it is always going to be wiser not to use questions in your essays; confine yourself to beautifully crafted and confident statements!

◼ Thesis statements

The thesis statement for your essay should be the last sentence of the introductory paragraph. It is possible to write a good essay with a more general statement at the beginning, so long as you build your argument to the thesis in the final paragraph. That structure can be quite difficult to manage, however, especially during a timed writing, so in most instances you will be wiser to begin with your thesis. You will see an example of the more sophisticated structure later in this chapter.

Here are some tips for writing a good thesis.

TIPS FOR WRITING

1   Write a statement that offers your interpretation of what the author's meaning is. That means that your thesis must make a claim about something the author believes, values, thinks or cares about.

2   The thesis must contain an idea which transcends the facts of the work. A sentence about the characters in a novel is not a thesis; the characters in the novel reveal something about human experience. Your thesis must state that broader idea.

3   The thesis must be a complete sentence.

4   The thesis should not contain a list of strategies. The analysis of the strategies belongs in your body paragraphs (see page 108) and should not begin in your introduction. The temptation to list some strategies can be strong but resist it. The list of strategies detracts from the idea around which you are organizing your essay.

5   Avoid the three-part thesis. Many students are taught to formulate thesis statements which contain three claims. An example of this type would be: 'In *The Great Gatsby*, Jay Gatsby is obsessed with Daisy, deluded about what he can accomplish and fails to achieve his goals.' Notice that this statement already violates point number two above, because it is about what a character is like, rather than about human experience in general. Notice also that if you wrote an essay on the basis of this thesis, it would end up being three separate little sections, independent of each other, and not really a unified essay at all. If you manage to write a thesis that has three parts, all of which are appropriately formatted as statements of ideas about human experience, you will simply have too much to do in your relatively short essay.

6   Be specific! Claiming that the author 'makes a point' about something is not a thesis. A general statement of topic is not a thesis.

ACTIVITY 5: EVALUATING THESIS STATEMENTS

Read each of the following proposed thesis statements and identify which of the numbered tips in the Tips for writing box it violates. Note that a statement might violate more than one of the recommendations! If the statement doesn't violate any, then it is a viable thesis. You can find the answers in the notes at the end of the book when you are done.

A   In 'Once More to the Lake', EB White shows that he loved the lake as a child.

B   In 'Once More to the Lake', EB White tells us about the lake he used to go to as a child, gives us details of what the lake was like then, and then gives us details of what the lake is like now.

C   In 'Once More to the Lake', EB White shows that the recognition of one's own mortality is a devastating experience that changes our vision of ourselves in a fundamental way.

D   In 'Once More to the Lake', EB White uses symbolism, flashback and anecdote to make his point.

E   In 'Once More to the Lake', EB White writes about death.

F   EB White's 'Once More to the Lake' shows that memory, nostalgia, confusion and death.

■ Analysis paragraphs

The body of your essay is where the analysis belongs. Analysis paragraphs have a very simple structure, with three parts, called **claim, evidence, warrant**. That structure is often abbreviated as **C-E-W**. The claim is the statement of what you intend to demonstrate in the paragraph, and the claim must tie directly back to the topic of the essay and your thesis statement. The evidence is the easiest part: the evidence is the stuff from the text, either quoted or paraphrased, which demonstrates the accuracy of your claim.

The following example paragraph comes from an essay written for a university essay contest for philosophy students. The separate sections of the argument – the claim, evidence and warrant, have been highlighted for you.

> KEY TERM
>
> C-E-W (claim, evidence, warrant) – the claim is the statement of what you intend to demonstrate in the paragraph, which ties back to the topic of the essay (the warrant). The evidence is the information from the text that supports the claim. The warrant is the explanation of your thinking.

The yellow section is the claim in the paragraph. The author asserts that there is an external reality outside of her mind. The rest of the paragraph, then, must provide the argument to support that claim.

The pink section is the warrant. Notice that it takes up just about half the entire paragraph. It explains why the evidence listed in the green section proves the claim in the yellow section.

Although we must acknowledge our inability to verify with absolute certainty the existence of a reality bigger than our minds, I believe in the existence of that reality nevertheless. My belief is a matter of pragmatism: Actions often result in predictable outcomes, and I have many times observed that people who fail to believe in those predictable outcomes have to suffer the consequences – usually negative – of that disbelief. The experience is a common one: if I let the water evaporate out of my vase of Valentine's Day roses, the roses will wilt. If I run headlong into a wall, the resulting crash will cause me pain. If I arrive at the airport half an hour after the time my flight was scheduled to leave, I will end up standing in the line for a ticket to a later flight, and, most likely, I will pay a fee to make that change. None of these events are susceptible to alteration by my simple desire for things to be different or by my belief that things are different. One might offer an argument that my pragmatic belief in reality is misplaced, because my internal reality is organized in such a way as to produce events and experiences over which I have no control and which operate on exactly the same principles as those I propose for the external reality that I only imagine exists; however, if that were the case, there would be no distinction between the two realities, internal and external. For all practical purposes, then, I believe that external reality has substance.

The green highlighting shows the evidence. This paragraph contains a rather unusual set of evidence; normally, you must include a warrant for each individual piece of evidence. In this case, however, each piece of evidence is like all the rest: all make exactly the same point; thus it is acceptable to list the evidence first and then evaluate it. Notice, too, that in this essay, the evidence is essentially hypothetical. It lists events that could happen but it does not refer to specific events that have already happened. That is acceptable in this medium, a philosophy essay, but hypothetical evidence is not going to be acceptable in most of your analysis essays, including those for English or for Theory of Knowledge.

As mentioned in the annotation above for this C-E-W example, normally you must write a warrant for each bit of evidence you include. You must not list several pieces of evidence and then try to tack the warrant on the end.

The most common mistake that beginning writers make when writing textual analysis is to leave off the warrant, or to include a warrant that is nowhere near detailed enough. You cannot make assumptions; you must spell out your whole line of thinking.

ACTIVITY 6: IDENTIFYING C-E-W IN A SAMPLE PARAGRAPH

The following paragraph was taken from a Theory of Knowledge essay. Read it and identify the claim (or claims), the evidence and the warrant(s). You might want to make a copy of the paragraph and then use three different colour highlighters to mark the various parts. When you have finished, you can read the activity notes at the end of the book.

Sometimes valuable discoveries are not made from deliberate investigation, but rather by chance. Andrew Nalbandov, who discovered that hypophysectomized chickens—chickens whose pituitary glands have been removed (Dixon 31)—died unless they
5   were exposed to a minimum of two one-hour periods of light nightly (Dixon 32). This discovery occurred as the result of a serendipitous event: a substitute janitor working at the research facility preferred to leave the lights on all night. By a second lucky chance, Nalbandov discovered the difference between this janitor's habits and those of
10 the regular janitor, and noted that while the substitute janitor was on duty, Nalbandov's chickens did not die (Dixon 32). The knowledge Nalbandov gained was invaluable to him—a string of dead chickens resulted only in negative knowledge and stalled the experiment—but it was not gained as the result of a difficult process. Luck is sometimes
15 a primary mechanism in the making of scientific knowledge, and often, as in this case and in the more famous case of the discovery of penicillin, the knowledge gained is highly valued, but not because of any particular difficulty in attaining it.

■ Conclusions

Conclusions are notoriously difficult to write, but that reputation is somewhat misleading. When one has written a strong, logical, coherent argument, the conclusion is often inevitable. In such a case, the conclusion is the paragraph which must be written to finish the job the essay set out to do. If, however, you find yourself in the position of not knowing quite what to do to finish your essay, you can try one of the following methods.

TIPS FOR WRITING
✔ Include a brief summary of the essay's main points.
✔ Ask a provocative question.
✔ Use a quotation.
✔ Evoke a vivid image.
✔ Call for some sort of action.
✔ End with a warning.
✔ Universalize (compare to other situations).
✔ Suggest results or consequences.

The most important characteristic of an effective conclusion is that it develops organically out of the essay. Think of a mathematical proof or a formal argument: you lay out the premises and then the conclusion is the inevitable implication of the fact that all those premises are true. The same must be true, of your essay: in the body, you lay out the conclusions you have drawn about the work of literature, and the best conclusion will be one which must inevitably follow from the basis you laid down.

■ Overall organization

The important thing to remember when you are planning your essay is that you are building an argument. Each of your analysis paragraphs is one premise in your argument, and the conclusion is that which must be true, now that you have demonstrated all the premises. You need to order the paragraphs in such a way that your reader follows your line of thinking: first, one must realize this, then this, then this and so on. If you have organized your essay well, the reader must read each paragraph in order to understand the paragraph that follows it.

The most common error that inexperienced writers make is to write separate paragraphs, all of which relate to the thesis and/or the topic of the essay, but which do not relate to each other. Your best tool for ensuring the interrelation of your paragraphs is the transitions between them. The transitions must provide an overt connection between the ideas in one paragraph to the ideas in the one that follows it.

Under no circumstance should you be aiming to write a five-paragraph essay. The five-paragraph essay is a beginner's structure; it's like having training wheels on your bicycle. By the time you reach your Diploma Programme course of study, you should be moving beyond those structures. Possibly, you might end up with an essay that happens to have five paragraphs, but you are much more likely to end up with an essay with more paragraphs – especially in the case of a comparison/contrast essay, as you will see later in the chapter.

■ Writing about unseen texts

In exam Paper 1, you will have to write about a text (or two texts at Higher Level) that you have not seen before. You will be working under timed conditions, so you will have to both study the text and plan and write the essay in the time allotted. You should assign about half of your time to the studying of the text and the planning of your essay and half the time to writing. If you are an HL student writing about two texts on Paper 1, you need to plan your time carefully. Allot half of the overall time to each text, and then half of that for planning and half for writing.

You will have questions that you can use to help guide you in your reading. The following tips will help you approach the task of writing about unseen texts effectively:

■ Plan your time carefully.

■ Read the text thoroughly at least twice. Consider the vocabulary carefully. Do you know all the words? If there are numerous words you don't know, especially in a poem, then you should not choose that text. If you are an HL student, of course, you do not have a choice, so you will need to work carefully with a text that has many unfamiliar words!

■ Read the questions and consider the text with them in mind.

■ Choose the aspects of the text that you want to write about. Make sure that you write about at least one element from the text for each of the requirements listed in the question. If there are several that are equally important, then choose the most sophisticated ones you can find.

■ Write the thesis statement before you write the introduction. In a timed writing, you do not need an elaborate introduction. If you are stuck for what to write as an introduction, leave some extra lines to add a paragraph later, write the thesis and go from there. You can go back and write the introduction at the end if you have time.

Sample Paper 1

The following sample includes analysis of two texts and is therefore similar to the guided analysis that HL students will have to produce for exam Paper 1. Standard level students will also have to do a guided analysis for Paper 1, but they will have to choose one of the two texts to write about. The following essays were written under timed conditions, and students did not have access to any background or contextual information. You will see from the comments that sample 1 has some flaws, particularly in the organization of the analysis paragraphs. The interpretations that the student has made also may not actually reflect what the creator of the diagram was thinking – the point is for the student to justify his or her interpretations with logical explanations. The essay is, nevertheless, a very fine paper and would earn high marks.

(Note about the guiding question: you will get a guiding question for each text on your exam Paper 1; however, it will not be compulsory for you to answer it. For the purposes of this model, the essay does directly respond to the guiding question.)

■ Text 1: You can view this text online by using the QR code

Note: a Sankey diagram is one in which the width of the flow bars, which represent data, is proportional depending on the percentage represented. So the wider bars represent the greatest percentage (Phineas).

Guiding question: A diagram does more than just present data; it shapes an interpretation of data. What stylistic techniques are significant in terms of creating meaning?

The Sankey diagram which portrays the subjects who have been attacked by Donald Trump on Twitter from January 20 to October 11 of 2017, a period of eight-and-a-half months, does more than just present data: it presents the data in such a way as to create a satire and a comment on Mr Trump's particular brand of ive.

The basis for the satire is the breakdown of the targets Trump has focused on, but the stylistic techniques highlight some points that help us understand the meaning inherent in the diagram. Symbolism is used in several ways. First of all, the medium of the Sankey diagram is a choice which helps us notice some striking points of data by examining the use of colour. Red and blue are colours which are cultural standards for representing the Republican and Democratic parties, respectively. A glance at the diagram reveals that Trump has attacked Democrats much more than Republicans – about three times as often. This particular idea is not a surprising one, as Trump was the Republican candidate, and so might be expected to be angrier at Democrats than at members of his own party. More surprising is the amount of purple, which we can see represents the media. Purple is, of course, a blend of red and blue, so purple could represent the idea that the media consists of both Republicans and Democrats. Because this is a Sankey diagram, the width of the media bar shows us at once that Trump has attacked the media in tweets far more often than he has attacked specific Democrats and Republicans together. He has attacked the media nearly twice as often as he has partisan politicians.

So far, the strategy of using colour would seem to function as a straight presentation of data without any kind of bias or commentary; however, the choice of purple for the media could actually reveal an interesting idea. Since the media are represented in purple, we can infer that the subjects of the media attacks were equally Republican and Democratic; however, if we examine the names of the specific news outlets that have been targeted, we can see that they are all outlets which are generally considered to be left-leaning, so we might conclude that Trump, at least, feels that he is attacking Democrats when he is attacking media. The use of purple offers a different perspective: that in attacking the news media, a president attacks all people, as the news media is a significant institution in terms of functioning to keep a government honest. The data and use of colour,

Left margin annotations:

This is the thesis statement. It gives a direct answer to the guiding question. The essay has, therefore, answered part of the guiding question – it identifies the point that the diagram makes. The rest of the essay must now support this claim.

Symbolism being used 'in several ways' is a claim, and the rest of the paragraph (or in this case, the next several paragraphs) must demonstrate that claim.

The green highlighting is the evidence. Evidence consists of facts; in this case, facts about standard symbolism and facts about relative quantity.

This paragraph has also been highlighted to demonstrate the claim-evidence-warrant structure.

Note that this piece of evidence requires the writer of the essay to know something about the cultural context from which this diagram has been created.

Right margin annotations:

This paragraph identifies the main stylistic technique employed in the diagram, so we already have a complete answer to the guiding question by the beginning of the second paragraph. Again, the rest of the essay must support the claims; the plain answer without evidence and support is insufficient.

In this essay, we have an overall claim – symbolism is used several ways – and we now expect a number of sub-claims, one for each of the different ways symbolism is used. The yellow text is the specific claim to be demonstrated in this paragraph.

All of this is warrant – explanation of how the facts about colour symbolism demonstrate the claim that colour symbolism makes 'striking' points – 'striking' suggests a degree of significance beyond the neutral.

Notice that the last part of this warrant connects the argument about the significance of colour symbolism to the original thesis, which claims that the diagram is satire.

In this paragraph, the writer has given multiple pieces of evidence. Each one is followed by an explanation – a warrant.

This paragraph begins with what will be the final sub-claim about the importance of symbolism: the symbol of the line indicating 'fake news'. The writer keeps the reader informed about how the argument is developing.

The connection to satire on Trump and his tweets is more direct here.

therefore suggest a satire on a president who does not wish to be monitored or reined in.

Another interesting symbolic element in this diagram is the use of spatial relationships. In the United States, the Republican Party is said to be the right-wing party, and the Democratic Party is said to be the left-wing party (hence the 'left-leaning' press mentioned above). In this diagram, the symbolism of the left and the right contribute to the idea that this diagram is a satire. We can see, first of all, that the media – the subject of Trump's greatest number of attacks, is positioned to his left-hand side. That could suggest that the media, for Trump, is a left-wing institution. As we have seen, the use of purple to represent the media counters that impression. We can also see that Trump holds his phone in his left hand, but that his Twitter finger, as it were, poised and ready to attack, is on his right hand. So we could therefore interpret the diagram as giving us an image of right ready to attack left.

A third interesting use of the right/left spatial relationship is the positioning of the red tie. Trump is famous for wearing an extra-long red tie, and the extreme length of the tie in the diagram is, by itself, a satire on those ties. The other interesting aspect of the tie, however, is that it seems to be growing longer and longer and moving further and further to the right. That image, then, implies that Trump's tweets are making the divide between left and right in the country more extensive and harder to mend.

A final important symbolic feature of this Sankey diagram is the line which is used to indicate Trump's attacks on 'fake news'. That line is, naturally, on the purple side of the diagram, but it stands out from the other media attacks and is heading in a different direction – straight out instead of up, as the rest of the purple flow is directed. If we look closely, we see that the attacks on 'fake news' comprise more than one-third of all attacks on media. There have, in fact, been more attacks on 'fake news' than on Republicans, Democrats, or 'others'. The irony is that, if one knows the context in which the tweets have been sent, one knows that what Trump labels 'fake news' is never fake news. Trump calls 'fake' anything which makes him look bad or which he does not wish to be true. Because the diagram isolates that particular data stream so that it stands out from all the others – and so that it heads a different direction – it calls attention to the fact that Trump attacks on an emotional, rather than a rational, basis.

The overall effect of the diagram, then, is satirical. The data is not simply presented in a neutral form. We can interpret the use of the Sankey format and the use of colour and spatial relationships to mean that Trump's

Here we have a new sub-claim about the use of symbolism. Colour has been dealt with; now the writer moves on to symbolic spatial relationships.

This particular connection back to the thesis is not as direct as the connection was in the previous paragraph. It might have been better phrased, but the idea is there: since the image makes a comment about the divide between right and left, the image is a satire. The writer of the essay could have made that idea more overt.

Here the writer mentions two more important elements of meaning in the diagram: irony and social context. The guiding question, which the writer has chosen to answer, asks for stylistic techniques, so the writer has focused on the main important stylistic technique, but the mention of two other important aspects of the diagram does reveal a sophisticated understanding of how the diagram communicates.

tweets are indicative of an unhealthy political discourse – if tweets can be called discourse! The diagram is not merely informational; it is social commentary.

The conclusion is fairly simplistic, in that it simply repeats what has been said before, but in a timed-writing situation, this kind of conclusion is satisfactory. It lays out the argument in simple terms and shows that the writer was in control of his or her developing thinking.

ACTIVITY 7: EVALUATING ANALYTICAL WRITING AND IDENTIFYING C-E-W

Read the essay below, which was written in response to the guiding question for Text 2 and then comment on its effectiveness, similar to the comments that were made for the Text 1 essay on the previous pages. Did the essay answer the question? Is the essay structured effectively, using the claim-evidence-warrant structure for the body paragraphs? Does the essay show good understanding of the text and of the task requirements? When you are finished, you can read the comments at the end of the book.

Text 2: 'Bill Stern: The Greatest Mythmaker of Them All' by Bill Bryson, Sr

The following extract has been taken from an article by American sports writer, Bill Bryson, Sr, who was renowned for his work in the mid-20th century. The original source of publication is unknown, but it was reprinted in a collection of his work put together by his son and grandson after his death.

Guiding question: Comment on the audience and purpose of this extract. Where relevant, discuss the stylistic features used to achieve the purpose.

Bill Stern was once considered the dean of American sportscasters. Unfortunately, that urgent, distinctive theatrical voice spun some of the biggest sports lies ever told. It will take historians a hundred years to expunge the myths Stern created from 1939 to 1951 in his 'Sports Newsreel' show.

5 His audience rating was among the highest in network radio. Bill used the suspense method to tell the wondrous deeds of some young athlete, keeping the identity a secret until the punchline: 'And that man was …' Here would come the name of any celebrity from Einstein to Eisenhower.

Stern never let a fact stand in the way of a dramatic climax. He wrenched history out of
10 shape to fit his script.

Those closely associated with sports all have their favorite Stern myth, and this is one of the favorites.

When Abraham Lincoln lay dying, Stern related, he sent for General Abner Doubleday, the man who was supposed to have invented baseball. And the president's last words were
15 addressed to the general: 'Keep baseball alive. In the trying days ahead, the country will need it.'

Aside from the facts that Lincoln never recovered consciousness after he was shot, and that Doubleday was nowhere around the death scene, the story is absolutely true.

This historical review by Bill Bryson, Sr has a somewhat unusual purpose, in that Bryson clearly intends to discredit someone who was a highly regarded celebrity in his day.

Bryson takes on Stern with very direct accusations, beginning with the title of the piece. To call Stern a 'mythmaker' might initially seem to be a flattering comment, especially since the modifier is 'the greatest ... of all,' but we quickly find out that Bryson does not intend flattery. In line 2, we are told directly that Stern was a liar, and in lines 3–4 Bryson points out that it will take a hundred years to eliminate those lies. The strategy of direct accusation is unusual in that we are more accustomed to people hedging with euphemisms. The blunt language immediately undercuts the somewhat romantic phrasing of the title and reveals Bryson's intention. The reliance on the blunt language, 'lies', in other words, suggests the degree to which Bryson is offended by their use and perpetuation.

Bryson goes on to use an anecdote to underscore his point. He tells the story that Stern told about Abraham Lincoln calling Abner Doubleday to his (Lincoln's) deathbed for the express purpose of trying to ensure that baseball will survive because baseball will somehow help the country get through the aftermath of the Civil War (lines 13–16). Stern's story is pretty outrageous in its own right. If his listeners knew anything about Lincoln's death, they knew that he never regained consciousness, as Bryson points out in line 17, and so the listeners would have known Stern for a liar immediately. Even if one does not know the actual history of Lincoln, the story is highly improbable – the idea that a president who has just seen the end of four years' of terrible warfare would think that baseball would be the country's salvation is just not believable. Bryson lets the story stand in its own right, in a separate paragraph, so that the ridiculousness of Stern's claim might sink in.

Bryson follows up that moment of reader thinking immediately, however, with a strong comment, so that no one might miss the point. In the final paragraph of the extract, Bryson uses sharp satire – even sarcasm – to show his disdain for Stern's fanciful version of historical events. 'Aside from the facts that Lincoln never recovered consciousness after he was shot, and that Doubleday was nowhere around the death scene, the story is absolutely true.' That 'the story is absolutely true' is strongly sarcastic because, of course, the two actual historical facts that Bryson provided in the early part of the sentence have already shown that nothing at all in Stern's story is true. By underscoring the facts with sarcasm, Bryson again shows his anger at Stern for making up history.

This short commentary by Bill Bryson reveals something important about the nature of the knowledge of history. Bryson's audience is others who think, as he does, that we have a moral obligation to record history as accurately as possible. He makes this point by giving us the example of Bill Stern, a person who ignored that obligation entirely and, in the name, apparently, of entertainment, made up whatever he wanted. While others might claim that Stern's story-telling is harmless, Bill Bryson, Sr obviously thinks differently: he believes that what Stern did for 12 years was a violation of the ethical pursuit of historical knowledge, and in this piece, he does his part to discredit someone who was once considered a star.

Comparison/contrast

KEY TERMS

Block-by-block – an essay technique whereby you write all your analysis of one work and then all your analysis of the other work.

Point-by-point – a technique in essay writing that takes each point and analyses how each one is used in both texts before you move on to the next point.

Exam Paper 2 will require you to write a comparison/contrast essay. The two ways to organize a comparison/contrast essay are called **block-by-block** and **point-by-point**. A block-by-block organizational structure is much less sophisticated than a point-by-point structure. If you are very short on time, you can use the block-by-block method, but even during the exam, you will show yourself to be a more sophisticated writer if you use the point-by-point method, so you should do so if you possibly can. If you are not writing under timed circumstances, you should not resort to block-by-block for any reason.

Block-by-block structure

The block-by-block structure looks just like it sounds: you write all your analysis of one work followed by all of your analysis of the other work. The problem with this structure is that it tends to turn into two miniature essays which don't really connect to each other. You end up with two essays which answer the question, but which do not show that you can really compare and contrast. Block-by-block structure looks like this:

- Introduction.
- Block one: all analysis of one work.
- Block two: all analysis of the second work.
- Conclusion.

■ Point-by-point organization

A point-by-point organization forces you to do the actual comparison/contrast work, because you must choose specific points to discuss about each work. Once you have chosen the main points of your argument, you bring them up one at a time and you analyse how each one is used in both texts before you move on to the next point of argument. Point-by-point structure looks like this:

- Introduction.

- Point one: work one.

- Point one: work two – this paragraph needs to contain an overt reference back to the previous paragraph, stating whether this work handles the technique in the same way as the first work or differently.

- Point two: work one.

- Point two: work two – this paragraph needs to contain an overt reference back to the previous paragraph, stating whether this work handles the technique in the same way as the first work or differently.

- (Add more alternating points as needed.)

- Conclusion.

You write two paragraphs for each point, one for each work, for however many points you are going to write about. You probably should not be trying for more than three different points in an essay, given the limitations you are under. Too many points mean superficial treatment of one or more of them. You can write an excellent essay with deep analysis of two different points of comparison and/or contrast. If your points are not extremely complicated, however, you should aim to make at least three points of connection between the two works.

■ Example: Point-by-point structure

The following sample essay is a good model of how to use this structure. The points around which the student has structured his analysis are:

- historical attitudes toward gender

- the contrast of older historical attitudes and structures with modernity.

This essay was also written under the pressure of time, and you will see that it is not perfect in terms of achieving all the goals laid out in this chapter; however, it is still very fine work. You do not have to be perfect. Strive to achieve all the objectives, but remember, you can still earn very high marks if you have a few relatively minor errors.

The student wrote a solid comparison/contrast essay in which he connects the two works to each other with regard to each point that he makes, so we, as readers, gain a clear sense of how the two works are alike and different in their handling of the topic that was assigned for the essay.

Writers often import or adapt historical material in writing their works. In at least two works you have studied, explore what or how this material contributes to the works.

'The Awakening' by Kate Chopin and 'The Great Gatsby' by F Scott Fitzgerald were published less than 30 years apart. Despite, however, their relative proximity in date of publication, they propose radically different portraits of contemporary America. Both Chopin and Fitzgerald use their texts to harshly critique the social attitudes and morals of the time, be they too rigid or too loose. They each effectively examine the historical attitudes in play shaping contemporary society and morality. 'The Awakening' takes place in 'turn of the century' Louisiana, a predominantly catholic and conservative state and emblematic of a fading social order in which women acted as the property of their husbands. 'The Great Gatsby' has come to define the so called 'Jazz age' of the 'Roaring' 1920s, marked by economic prosperity, unrestrained consumerism, and rapidly crumbling post-war social morals. Here, the society in question appears to be lurching forward to the future whereas 'The Awakening's Louisiana seems to cling to the past. This essay will explore, with reference to gender roles and social structure, how Chopin and Fitzgerald use historical material (namely preserved attitudes) as a foil for the more modernist and progressive forces shaping each story.

Gender is a compelling element of both texts. While Edna in 'The Awakening' promotes a highly progressive vision of womanhood and female autonomy, her counterpart Daisy, in 'The Great Gatsby' appears to reject the 'looser' morals of the society around her to cling onto a perhaps more historical notion of devoted loyalty to husband and child. The primary conflict within Chopin's 'The Awakening' is Edna's struggle to liberate herself from the oppressive gender expectations placed upon her. These expectations and limits are stressed by the bird imagery running throughout. Birds, traditional symbols of freedom through flight, are kept in cages for human pleasure. Like the birds, Edna feels entrapped within a context of unchanging social attitudes. Her independence and movements are limited and she, like Madame Lebrun's parrot, is unable to effectively communicate. In the New Orleans social world in which the novel is set, femininity is severely dictated and governed. A woman is expected to act as a loving daughter, wife and mother, with no recognition of her own sexuality. The women surrounding Edna (such as Mme Ratignolle) appear to embrace their outlined social role: 'They were women who idolised their children, worshipped their husbands, and esteemed it a holy privilege to effect themselves as individuals and grow wings as ministering angels'. These 'angels' use their wings to protect and administer care rather than fly. Edna comes to understand that her husband considers her 'a valuable piece of personal property'. These rigid social attitudes can be considered historical in that they are preserved from the past without discernible change. Edna, in contrast, develops a heightened awareness of her status in the world and attempts to reject it to 'free her soul from responsibility'. She abandons her husband and two sons and personally instigates affairs (one sexual with Alcee, and one emotional with Robert). In this, her modern ideas about womanhood clash with the historical attitudes towards womanhood of the society to which she belongs.

'The Great Gatsby' also considers gender politics (though to a lesser extent) in its portrait of the roaring twenties. While the women here are perhaps 'freer' than those featured in 'The Awakening', they are still bound by social constraints that the male characters are able to avoid. The primary female characters: Daisy, Jordan and Myrtle, are all to some extent defined by their relationships to the male characters in the story. This can be observed by the casual fashion by which Nick refers to Tom and Daisy: 'I drove over there to have dinner with the Tom Buchanans', Tom's identity encompasses his wife. At Gatsby's party, Nick observes the 'men and girls' (using the term girls rather than women). These details can be appreciated as remnant of historical attitudes and practices governing society despite the widespread modernisation of many other societal elements. 1920s New York appears somewhat accepting of sexual liberalism (the difference can be visualized when women attend Gatsby's parties sporting revealing outfits). Tom openly engages in a sexual affair with his mistress Myrtle, without remarkable retribution or consequence. Daisy also lacks serious hesitation before rehabilitating her romantic relationship with Jay Gatsby. However, despite her affair, Daisy retains a historically inspired attitude towards female duty. She eventually decides to remain in a marital union with Tom rather than leave him for Jay. In this, she rejects the progressive attitude that Edna pushed for and embraced. She hopes that her daughter be 'a fool – that's the best thing a girl can be in this world, a beautiful little fool'. Daisy thus promotes a patriarchal vision of the female ideal as ditzy and beautiful, oblivious of social entrapment and 'gilded cages'.

In addition to gender, the two texts also foil preserved historical structures and attitudes with modernity when it comes to societal structure and materialism. 'The Awakening's' New Orleans possesses a deeply entrenched class system reminiscent of historical divides that Edna appears to snub when she rejects huge wealth to live alone in a cottage: 'There was with her a feeling of having descended in the social scale, with a corresponding sense of having risen in the spiritual.' Edna thus rejects the security of her position at the top of the historic class structure just as she rejects its oppressive nature, she identifies an inverse relationship between social rank and liberation/independence. This proves her character to be unfazed by social materialism and thus socially progressive. She recognizes that her value is not linked to wealth or status. Chopin employs the motif of houses to emphasize this rebuke of historically valued wealth and class. Edna stays in multiple houses in the course of the story (in the Grand Isle cottages, the large family home in New Orleans and finally her 'pigeon house'). Each of these homes can be seen as a marker of her emotional awakening as well as her shifting social status. The most significant shift takes place when Edna moves from her family's large New Orleans home to a much smaller cottage. This move can be seen as an attempted liberation from the plethora of Leonce's material objects with which Edna ultimately equates herself. In this move, Edna's progressivist ideas come into play and historical priorities are dismissed.

'The Great Gatsby' also approaches class and material success from a lens of conflict between history and modernity, as seen in the clash between 'Old Money' and 'New Money', personified by Tom Buchanan and Jay Gatsby. Fitzgerald stresses the division of the classes through setting and imagery. House locations in 'West Egg' and 'East Egg' respectively signify 'New and Old Money'. Similarly to Chopin, Fitzgerald uses the motif of houses as markers of social order. The rapid modernisation and economic boom driving the east coast New York's rampant consumerism divides the wealthy class into the historical 'old money' families with fortunes built up over hundreds of years alongside influential social connections with the newly developing 'new money' class who made their money in the 1920s boom and thus compensate for their lack of historical social status with lavish exhibitions of wealth. Gatsby's 'new money' is a key component of his identity and his insecurities and this class rivalry of the wealthy is a key underlying theme in the struggle over Daisy. Materialism also plays a major role in 'The Great Gatsby'. While Edna is repelled by the concept of being a man's possession and dismissive of the wealth and materialism, Daisy finds wealth alluring and attractive. She conflates her attraction to Gatsby with attraction to his newfound wealth and status, this conflation is best observed when she breaks down at the sight of Gatsby's luxurious and extensive collection of English shirts as well as through the superfluous and continuous luxury imagery. Daisy embraces the historical concept of selecting a partner for material gain and security. She ultimately envisions herself as a possession of Tom's.

'The Awakening' and 'The Great Gatsby', while they promote fundamentally disparate portrayals of America, are each decisively influenced by the societal context and culture in which their stories take place. Chopin and Fitzgerald, each in their treatment of context, consider the clash of historical material with the more modernist progression of either the protagonist or society itself. These contrasting attitudes and perceptions succeed in constructing a more nuanced vision of the characters as well as the macro societal shifts and evolution at large, thus enabling the reader to fully appreciate each story and each character's actions.

Ten tips for improving your writing style

1   Make sure that whatever subject you choose for your sentences can do the verb that you attach to it. Inexperienced writers often associate active verbs to non-sentient subjects, which results in false statements. For example: the sentence, 'Poetry understands that symbols can have flexible meanings', is not a true statement. Poetry cannot understand anything; readers can understand and poets can understand. Ensure that as many of your sentences as possible have people as subjects – the author, the narrator or speaker, the characters in the text and the readers should be the focus of your analysis, not abstractions.

2   Related to number one is the problem of passive voice and overuse of 'be' verbs. No form of the verb 'to be' is an action; 'to be' is just to exist. The 'be' verbs are: is, am, are, was, were, be, being and been. An essay filled with lots of instances of things existing is a very flat essay. Passive verbs nearly always use some form of the verb 'to be' as well, and you can see, just from the name, that nothing happens when you use the passive voice. Note the difference between the following two sentences:

   ■   The metaphor of the green light is used to show how Gatsby is in love with Daisy who is, to his mind, far away from him.

   ■   Fitzgerald uses the metaphor of the green light to embody Gatsby's obsession with Daisy, whom he sees as a distant, but highly desirable, objective.

   The second version is a much more powerful sentence. The verbs actually reveal a more sophisticated understanding, both of how the author uses the metaphor and of Gatsby's feeling for Daisy. Once you finish your first draft, go back and eliminate every 'be' verb that you can.

3   Make sure that you are precise in identifying subjects of sentences. 'This', 'that', 'these' and 'those' are not nouns; they are demonstrative pronouns. Every time you write one of those words, you must include the noun to which it refers. Many inexperienced writers tend to fill their sentences with statements like, 'This shows what the poet meant.' Such a sentence does not demonstrate your understanding of the text at all. You need to write something much more specific such as: 'This contradiction creates a juxtaposition that we would not ordinarily expect, and so reveals the author's intention to startle the reader with a new insight.'

4 Rely on nouns and verbs to carry your meaning; eliminate adjectives and adverbs as much as possible. Sometimes you will absolutely need an adjective so as, for example, to differentiate between two objects, but most adjectives end up being nothing but fluff. Read the following sample paragraph and notice how little is added to the actual analysis by the adjectives and adverbs.

This is the excellent and interesting opening paragraph of Jane Austen's most famous novel 'Pride and Prejudice', a novel about whether it is even really possible for most normal individuals to transcend rigid and unfair social expectations and make a highly successful marriage on their own personal and private terms. These first fascinating sentences are widely, famously renowned for their extremely clever wit, but they also slightly suggest a surprisingly wide range of interesting, deep philosophical possibilities, and perhaps it is that, as much as the engaging humour, which appeals. These two short sentences, only 71 words, reflect deep ideas not only about extreme wealth and successful marriage, but also about free will, individual selfhood and the deep meaning or pointless meaninglessness of life.

If you read carefully, you will see that the highlighted words are mostly redundant, or they pile on extra words that add nothing to the point that the paragraph makes. Now read the revised version from which the excess words have been eliminated.

This is the opening paragraph of Jane Austen's 'Pride and Prejudice', a novel about whether it is possible for individuals to transcend social expectations and make a successful marriage on their own terms. These first sentences are renowned for their wit, but they also suggest a surprising range of philosophical possibilities, and perhaps it is that, as much as the humour, which appeals. These two sentences, only 71 words, reflect ideas not only about wealth and marriage, but also about free will, selfhood and the meaning or meaninglessness of life.

This version is much cleaner. All the words are necessary for the point to be made. Look, particularly, at the use of the phrase 'free will': if you leave out the adjective 'free' there, the meaning changes significantly. 'Free' here is a necessary adjective. Remove all the clutter from your writing that you possibly can. Examiners will certainly know if you are trying to pad out your word count with essentially useless words.

5 Use the word 'it' as seldom as possible. Never use 'it' without a clear antecedent, unless it is in an idiom, such as 'it is raining'. If you cannot identify the antecedent for 'it', neither can the examiner. 'It' all by itself has no meaning, and if your essay gets filled up with lots of instances of 'it' without antecedents, you will find that the essay has little substance. The more specific and concrete you can be in your statements the better.

6 Equally problematic, though for different reasons, is the reliance on the pronoun 'you'. In spoken English, especially colloquial English, people often use 'you' to mean something like 'everyone' or 'anyone'. In writing, however, 'you' is a direct address to the reader. When we have said 'you' in this book, we have meant, specifically, you – the person reading the book. We are offering you, individually, advice. If you try to use 'you' in analytical writing, however, you will end up telling your reader (often an IB examiner) what he or she thinks or feels or does. If you do that, you run the risk of causing offence by ascribing to the reader a feeling he or she does not have, or you make untrue statements. Be sure that your pronouns properly identify the actual person who thinks, feels or acts the way that your sentence claims that he or she does.

7   Work hard on writing actual transitions, rather than relying on shortcuts such as 'to begin' or 'next' or 'similarly'. Writers who rely on one-word or simplistic transitions are using a shortcut which allows them to avoid doing the hard work of thinking about how two sentences or two paragraphs relate to each other in a meaningful way. Consider the difference between these two pairs of sentences:

Pair 1: These are the last sentence of one paragraph and the first sentence of the next paragraph. Notice that the 'next' does not help you, as a reader, to understand the relationship between the two paragraphs.

The blunt language immediately undercuts the somewhat romantic phrasing of the title and reveals Bryson's intention. The reliance on the blunt language, 'lies', in other words, suggests the degree to which Bryson is offended by their use and perpetuation.
Next, Bryson talks about Abraham Lincoln.

We don't know why Abraham Lincoln is relevant to the idea of blunt language.

Pair 2: These are the same two sentences, but now the first sentence of the new paragraph has been rewritten so that the relationship between the paragraphs is clear:

The blunt language immediately undercuts the somewhat romantic phrasing of the title and reveals Bryson's intention. The reliance on the blunt language, 'lies', in other words, suggests the degree to which Bryson is offended by their use and perpetuation.
Bryson goes on to use an anecdote about Abraham Lincoln to underscore his point.

This time, we can see that Abraham Lincoln is not the focus of the sentence, 'anecdote' is. Anecdote is a literary strategy, so that we see that where the previous paragraph talked about the literary strategy of blunt language, this paragraph is going to talk about another literary strategy.

8   Use punctuation correctly. Semi-colons must be used to join two independent clauses (complete sentences) or between items on a list. Commas are possibly the most frequently misused punctuation mark. Here are three rules for using commas that cover most (though definitely not all!) situations in which you need to use commas. If you follow these three rules, you will use commas correctly almost all the time.

   ✓ Use a comma when you are joining two independent clauses (sentences) with a coordinating conjunction (and, or, or but). Example: 'I wrote my English essay, and then I went running.'

   ✓ Use a comma after introductory elements. Example: 'Yesterday, when I went to the store, I bought milk.'

   ✓ Use two commas when you are using a non-restrictive element. That is, you use commas to set off a descriptive phrase that applies to all the objects in question. Example: 'The band members, who wore raincoats, did not get wet.' This sentence means that none of the band members got wet, because all of them were wearing raincoats. If you leave the commas out, you suggest that some of the band members were wearing raincoats and some were not, and only those who were not wearing the raincoats got wet. The commas change the meaning of the sentence entirely.

Improved use of commas in almost all situations will make your writing much clearer. You can develop a more sophisticated understanding of other situations in which commas might be used as you become a more sophisticated writer.

9   Eliminate pretentious vocabulary and say what you mean in a straightforward way. There is no need to use 'utilize' when 'use' will do. 'Implement' has a particular meaning; 'implement' is not an effective synonym for 'use'. Use 'implement' when you actually mean that someone has conceived a new way of doing something and is putting it into practice for the first time. When you rely too much on pretentious vocabulary, you run the risk of actually saying something that is not true (because you don't really understand the nuances of the words you are using) and/or of making yourself look, to an examiner, like someone trying to show off, rather than someone who makes a real effort to write precisely and accurately.

10 Write simple, direct sentences. When you have finished writing your essay, read it out loud – or recruit someone to read it out loud to you. You will hear problems that you did not read, especially problems of long, convoluted sentences which change direction mid-stream so that the subjects you started with don't go with the verbs you ended up with. (Obviously you cannot do this in a test situation!)

Conclusion

You will have to write about literary and non-literary texts quite often over the course of your IB English programme. You will have to write about different types of works, and you will have to address a variety of different questions about literature. This chapter has offered you quite a lot of advice about how to handle many aspects of that complex task. Try not to expect too much of yourself too soon. You will need to practise each skill over time in order to develop your ability. The ability to write is not an inborn skill: writers become better with practice. So practise, practise, practise! It is also well worth remembering that good writers are good readers. People who expose themselves to lots of good writing gradually internalize a great understanding of how effective language works. So along with practising your writing, read, read, read!

Additional resources

An excellent book for helping you write more clearly and succinctly is William Zinsser's *On Writing Well*. Finally, you might want to check out some good practical advice on how to write conclusions from the Writing Center at Harvard University: **https://writingcenter.fas.harvard.edu/pages/ending-essay-conclusions**

Works cited

Austen, Jane (1813), *Pride and Prejudice*, Clare West, ed., Oxford University Press, Oxford, 2008 (print).

Ballou, Sullivan, 'The Sullivan Ballou Letter', Ken Burns, ed., PBS: Public Broadcasting Service, *The Civil War*, 2015, Web, accessed 21 December 2018, **www.pbs.org/kenburns/civil-war/war/historical-documents/sullivan-ballou-letter/**

Bryson, Bill Sr, *The Babe Didn't Point and Other Stories About Iowans and Sports*, Michael G Bryson and Michael G Bryson, eds., Iowa State University Press, Ames IA, 1989 (print).

Chatwin, Bruce, *The Songlines*, Picador, New York, 1987 (print).

Chopin, Kate, *The Awakening*. Wilder Publications, Radford VA, 2018 (print).

Curtis, George William, 'Ebb and Flow', Bartleby.com, Web, accessed 21 December 2018, **www.bartleby.com/248/511.html**

Demby, Gene, 'That Cute Cheerios Ad With The Interracial Family Is Back', *NPR Code Switch: Race and Identity Remixed*, NPR.org, 30 January 2014, Web, accessed 23 December 2018, **www.npr.org/sections/codeswitch/2014/01/30/268930004/that-cute-cheerios-ad-with-the-interracial-family-is-back**

Dixon, Bernard, *What Is Science for?*, Harper & Row, New York, 1974 (print).

Fitzgerald, F Scott (1925), *The Great Gatsby*, Scribner, New York, 1995 (print).

Historynet.com, 'Sullivan Ballou: The Macabre Fate of an American Civil War Major.' *Historynet.com*, World History Group, 12 June 2006, Web, accessed 21 December 2018, www. historynet.com/sullivan-ballou-the-macabre-fate-of-a-american-civil-war-major.htm

Kight, Stef W, and Lazario Gamio, 'Who Trump Attacks the Most on Twitter', *Axios*, 14 October 2017, Web, accessed 26 December 2018, www.axios.com/who-trump-attacks-the-most-on-twitter-1513305449-f084c32e-fcdf-43a3-8c55-2da84d45db34.html#main

King George VI of Great Britain, 'The King Speaks: There May Be Dark Days Ahead', *Ibiblio. org*, Web, accessed 24 December 2018, www.ibiblio.org/pha/policy/1939/1939-09-03b.html

KSTP, 'Controversial CHEERIOS Commercial', YouTube, 2 June 2013, Web, accessed 23 December 2018, www.youtube.com/watch?v=pbWeH9cztHw

Ma, Alexandra, and Samantha Lee, 'This Diagram Shows Exactly How the Thai Soccer Team Was Rescued from the Cave', *Business Insider*, Insider, Inc., 10 July 2018, Web, accessed 23 December 2018, www.thisisinsider.com/how-thai-soccer-team-were-rescued-out-of-tham-luang-cave-diagram-2018-7

Neilson, John Shaw, 'The Girl with the Black Hair', *Collected Poems*, Lothian Book Publishing Company, Melbourne, 1934, Web, accessed 22 December 2018, www.poetrylibrary.edu.au/poets/neilson-john-shaw/poems

Neilson, John Shaw, 'May', *Collected Poems*, Lothian Book Publishing Company, Melbourne, 1934, Web, accessed 22 December 2018, www.poetrylibrary.edu.au/poets/neilson-john-shaw/poems

Nordquist, Richard, 'E.B. Whites's Drafts of "Once More to the Lake"', ThoughtCo.com, Dotdash Publishing Company, 2 September 2018, Web, accessed 24 December 2018, www.thoughtco.com/e-b-whites-drafts-once-more-1692830

Oluo, Ijeoma, 'Colin Kaepernick's National Anthem Protest Is Fundamentally American, *The Guardian*, Guardian News and Media, 29 August 2016, Web, accessed 22 December 2018, www.theguardian.com/commentisfree/2016/aug/29/colin-kaepernick-national-anthem-protest-fundamentally-american

Osundare, Niyi, 'Hole in the Sky', *Two Poems by Niyi Osundare*, *World Literature Today*, 15 September 2014, Web, accessed 23 December 2018, www.worldliteraturetoday.org/2014/may-august/two-poems-niyi-osundare

Phineas, 'Sankey Diagrams Blog - A Sankey Diagram Says More than 1000 Pie Charts.' *Sankey Diagrams*, Word Press, 21 December 2018, Web, accessed 23 December 2018, www.sankey-diagrams.com/

Rao, TS Sathyanarayana and Chittaranjan Andrade, 'The MMR vaccine and autism: Sensation, refutation, retraction, and fraud', *Indian Journal of Psychiatry*, PMC: US National Library of Medicine National Institutes of Health, April–June 2011, Web, accessed 23 December 2018, www.ncbi.nlm.nih.gov/pmc/articles/PMC3136032/

Shakespeare, William, *Romeo and Juliet*, Rebecca Niles and Michael Poston, eds., *Folger Digital Texts*, Folger Shakespeare Library, Web, accessed 23 December 2018, www.folgerdigitaltexts. org/?chapter=5&play=Rom&loc=p7

Snyder, John, 'Cashing in on Fear: The Danger of Dr. Sears', *Science-Based Medicine*, Digital Gravity Media, 7 March 2018, Web, accessed 23 December 2018, https://sciencebasedmedicine.org/cashing-in-on-fear-the-danger-of-dr-sears/

Vaccines ProCon.org', 'Should any vaccines be required for childen?', 23 July 2018, Web, accessed 23 December 2018, https://vaccines.procon.org/

Whitehead, Colson, *The Underground Railroad: a Novel*, Anchor Books, a division of Penguin Random House, New York, 2018 (print).

Notes on the activities

For most of these activities, there are no 'right' answers. The notes given here offer one way each of the activities might have been approached, but none is comprehensive. Use them to explore some possibilities of analysis or to open up discussion with your classmates.

You may very well have identified valid points about the various texts which are not covered in the notes. That does not mean that you are 'wrong'. If you have thought carefully and can back up your interpretations logically using the text, then your interpretation is likely to be just as viable as those given here. If you missed a lot of the ideas here, do not let yourself get discouraged: good analysis requires practice, and if you learned something about what *not* to do when working on analysis, then you learned something just as valuable as learning what you *should* do.

Chapter 2: Approaches to non-literary texts

■ Activity 1: Detecting bias

The two stories are both focused on the same event and come from the same source (the Associated Press). However, you should have noticed several differences in how the language of each article presents the issue. There are many examples of how these differences highlight bias, but if we focus just on the headlines, we can note the following:

The *Daily Mail*'s headline begins by stating that a 'caravan of migrants swells to 7 000 and stretches more than a mile long'. Putting a specific figure on the crowd's size, though not strictly hyperbole, does magnify its effect; quantifying a crowd of that size elicits fear and creates mob-like associations. The word 'migrant' is also a loaded word which carries negative associations for some people. 'Swells' is also used in *The Guardian* article, but the overall tone is very different from the *Daily Mail* article. In addition, the caravan of migrants does not just walk towards the border; instead, 'they continue marching towards the US border', which suggests an attitude of military-like defiance. Lastly, the headline includes a 'warning' from Trump, which further emphasizes the imminent threat posed by the 'onslaught of illegal aliens'.

The Guardian's headline is much shorter. The use of the word 'desperate' evokes a sense of pity in the audience, and the word 'refugee' suggests that the people in the caravan are victims, downplaying the threat that is suggested in the *Daily Mail* article. These 'refugees', in contrast to the 'migrants' of the *Daily Mail* article, are not 'marching towards' (or even 'making their way towards') the US; rather, they 'crossed into Mexico via the river'. 'Crossed into' is a much more neutral phrase, and there is no reference to nearing the US border, which lessens the 'threat' suggested in the *Daily Mail* article. Finally, including the image of the refugees crossing by river suggests that they are in danger, rather than suggesting that they themselves are the danger.

■ Activity 2: Considering historical context

In order to fully understand and appreciate this text, you would need to know a little bit about Wilfred Owen. Owen is one of the most celebrated First World War poets, perhaps best known for his poem 'Dulce et Decorum Est' which presents a bitter and cynical view of war. Owen fought on the Western Front in France and was killed just four days after he wrote this letter – exactly one week before the war ended – which makes this letter all the more poignant.

■ Activity 3: Considering target audience

The first thing that you may have noticed when examining the layout and design of this text is the use of colour. The bright blue and yellow colour tones create a cheerful and energetic mood, which is particularly engaging for a young audience. The pictures and other graphics, video, interactive elements and links, sidebar options, comprehension questions, vocabulary game and student comments all make for an exciting and accessible text which appeals to a younger audience.

The highlighted vocabulary also appeals to the younger demographic: we cannot tell from the text here, but it is likely that the highlighted text is hyperlinked (further investigation reveals that this is the case). This technique appeals to the different ability levels of the audience as those who may be unfamiliar with certain terminology can simply click on the link to see the definition or explanation of the word or phrase without disrupting the flow of the main text.

The 'tears of joy' emoji that is included in the still image from the video at the end of the article (and in the image earlier on) adds a humorous touch; it is almost as if the image itself reflects the overall tone of the article: elation over having been chosen as 'word' of the year.

■ Activity 4: Interpreting propaganda

Personal interpretations of this text will vary based on your own contextual circumstances. We could say that most people in a modern Western audience might first be drawn to the woman's appearance. With visible makeup and a very tidy hairstyle, she does not fit the stereotype of a soldier. Some further research into the context of production reveals the following:

> Bradshaw Crandell was well known for his cover-girl illustrations for *Cosmopolitan* magazine. Here he lends the same glamorous appeal to the Women's Army Corps. Posters such as this sought to reassure society that women would not lose their femininity by putting on a uniform. They maintained a stylistic continuity with familiar commercial images of women. This reinforced the government's stance that wartime occupations were temporary and would not fundamentally change women's traditional roles.
>
> Source: V&A Search the Collections

Modern attitudes to women in the armed forces are vastly different from the one presented here: women are given far more equal treatment, and recruitment posters do not emphasize appearances over actions.

The slogan at the top of the poster also has a different impact on a modern Western audience than it would have had on its contemporary audience. 'Are you a girl with a Star-Spangled Heart?' The word 'girl' could be considered patronizing when used to refer to a grown woman. Equally, the emphasis on the girl's 'heart' focuses attention on her femininity. 'Heart' is also an abstract word, which is perhaps a way of distancing women from the more concrete, active type of involvement in the army that men would have been recruited for.

■ Activity 5: Comparing registers

The language of the blog is much less formal than the essay. Due to the 'public' aspect of the blog, the author is very aware of her audience; thus, the style is almost conversational. Sentences are mainly short, simple and declarative (with one example of a rhetorical question thrown in).

■ Activity 6: The language of manifestos

The Women's Equality Party makes clever use of its abbreviation: 'WE' serves as both an acronym and an example of inclusive language. Each point reads as if the audience is involved in the proposed policies.

Repetition in the form of enumeration (specifically, triples) is also included in the manifesto:

'WE will implement <u>full-time</u>, <u>high quality</u>, <u>free</u> childcare for all children from the end of shared parental leave.'

'WE will put <u>prevention, protection and provision</u> at the heart of all our policies …' Note the use of alliteration here, which adds a rhythmic effect to the statement.

'<u>WE will</u> build an immigration system with gender equality and social justice at its heart. <u>WE will</u> design trade deals that work for everybody. <u>WE will</u> make sure Brexit does not turn back the clock on gender equality through secondary legislation.'

■ Activity 7: Rhetorical and figurative devices

Obama's speech is full of rhetorical and figurative devices, so much so that you could write a whole dissertation on their effects. An annotation of the first section is provided here:

Obama achieves many things in the opening of his speech:
1) He makes a direct address to the audience, establishing a bond.
2) He uses triples ('who still doubts', 'who still wonders', 'who still questions') to emphasize his point: that his victory is every American's victory.
3) He makes a subtle allusion to another famous speech: Martin Luther King, Jr's 'I Have a Dream' speech.

This phrase is repeated three times: an example of triples and of parallel structure.

Finally, Obama almost personifies change: change is not simply a passive agent but a powerful force that makes a grand entrance.

If there is anyone out there who still doubts that America is a place where all things are possible; who still wonders if the dream of our founders is alive in our time; who still questions the power of our democracy, tonight is your answer.

It's the answer told by lines that stretched around schools and churches in numbers this nation has never seen; by people who waited three hours and four hours, many for the very first time in their lives, because they believed that this time must be different; that their voice could be that difference.

It's the answer spoken by young and old, rich and poor, Democrat and Republican, black, white, Latino, Asian, Native American, gay, straight, disabled and not disabled – Americans who sent a message to the world that we have never been a collection of Red States and Blue States: we are, and always will be, the United States of America.

It's the answer that led those who have been told for so long by so many to be cynical, and fearful, and doubtful of what we can achieve to put their hands on the arc of history and bend it once more toward the hope of a better day.

It's been a long time coming, but tonight, because of what we did on this day, in this election, at this defining moment, change has come to America.

Here, Obama uses enumeration to build up to his point that each of the individual members of his audience (many of whom would be represented in that list) form part of the United States of America.

Inclusive language ('we') reinforces the bond that Obama created at the beginning of the speech.

Again, Obama uses triples to emphasize the historical significance of this election.

■ Activity 8: Textual features of an opinion column

An opinion column is defined by the following characteristics, which you will hopefully have emulated in your own opinion column in the creative extension part of the activity:

- A clear argument in response to a timely, often controversial, issue.

- Specific references to facts, data or anecdotal evidence to strengthen the argument.

- Acknowledgement of the counterargument, which is refuted with facts.

- Stylistically, an opinion column will usually begin with an attention-grabber and end with a thought-provoking line or a call to action.

- Clear, concise language which is free of jargon or complex terminology.

- Persuasive techniques.

- A distinctive voice.

In their 'How to write' guide in *The Guardian*, Peter Cole and Michael White put it like this:

> The good column will have a clear identity, so that the readers will feel they know the writer, his or her prejudices, enthusiasms and obsessions. The best columns inform the opinions of the readers; the best 'me' columns are retold by their readers as though they are gossiping about friends.

Chapter 3: Approaches to literary texts

■ Activity 1: 'The Tell-Tale Heart' by Edgar Allan Poe

The narrator's paranoia is the clue that he is not to be relied upon. He begins the story by admitting that he is nervous, which is not a guarantee of unreliability, but he goes right on to defend himself against a charge, which was apparently made just prior to the start of the story, that he is insane. Despite his claim that he can tell us his story calmly, his claim that he can hear 'all things in heaven and earth' and 'many things in hell' tells us that he is, indeed, insane. No one can do what he claims he can do. Poe has signalled to us right from the first paragraph of the story that we are dealing with an unreliable narrator.

■ Activity 2: Shakespeare's Sonnet 73

First metaphor: tenor = old age; vehicle = a tree in winter.

The characteristics of the tree which Shakespeare points out are:

- the bareness of the boughs

- the shaking of the boughs in the cold

- the emptiness of the boughs where birds used to sit and sing.

All three of these features can be applied to the man's body – we can see that Shakespeare wants us to understand that the life (the birds singing) is going out of the body, and that it now trembles in the cold weather – or the cold of approaching death. The limbs are bare; hair no longer grows there and we can imagine the arms and legs shrivelling.

Second metaphor: tenor = old age; vehicle = twilight.

The characteristics of the twilight which Shakespeare points out are:

- that this is the moment of twilight immediately after the light has faded from the west
- that full dark is only moments away
- that night is like death.

We understand from this metaphor that Shakespeare wants us to understand that the man has reached the very end of his life. The light has gone out of it, and he is only moments (possibly days, translated into terms of a life rather than of a single day) from death. He is very aware that the full darkness of death is about to take him. This metaphor makes death seem much closer than the first metaphor did – while it was winter in the first quatrain, the suggestion is that there are possibly a few yellow leaves left on the tree. Here, we are pointed to the moment of a day when the sun has disappeared below the horizon, just before full darkness.

Third metaphor: tenor = old age; vehicle = dying fire.

The characteristics of the dying fire that Shakespeare points out are:

- what is left is the glowing embers on ashes
- what remains of the fire is that which is being consumed – the same thing that used to nourish it. In other words, we are asked to think about the fact that wood and oxygen nourish a fire, but once the wood is gone, and only embers remain, the oxygen will suffocate the fire.

This image of the dying fire gives us the understanding that the narrator of the poem is beyond recovering. His death is inevitable. The only way to stoke up a fire is to add more wood, and no one can add restored youth to an old man. We also understand that he has regrets – he used to be nourished by the experience of living, but now each day drains him further.

■ Activity 3: *'Master Harold' … and the boys*

The symbolism of Hally coming inside out of the rain is a symbol of coming out of danger into security. At the end of the play, however, he goes back out into the storm. That suggests that he is going back out into danger. We get from that a sharp contrast between inside and outside, and perhaps the fact that he has gone back out again might suggest that something has gone wrong inside to make inside not such a safe place any more. We might also consider the idea of rebirth: perhaps we will find that this character is in some way made new by coming in out of the rain at the beginning. At the end, though, he is going into the water, and we don't see him emerging from it. Perhaps the opportunity is there for change, but we don't know what will become of that chance.

■ Activity 4: 'The Prodigal' by Elizabeth Bishop

Typically we would expect morning to be time for a new start, a rebirth, and night time to be a time of danger or impending death. Since we know that this character is an alcoholic, and that he drinks at night, the morning would seem to be the chance for rebirth. Night time is presented here as a time of warning, so we might think that the danger is his drinking.

If you noticed those patterns, you have done well. If you read the entire poem, however, you would discover that Bishop has upended the traditional symbolism. It turns out that what morning reassures him about is that he can go right on drinking, and that the warning that comes at night is the sense that he has to face the truth and deal with the drinking problem.

One other element you might have noticed is the religious allusion to the story of the prodigal son from the Christian Bible. The prodigal son left home, spent a fortune and got himself into a lot of trouble. When he went home again, he was welcomed by his forgiving father. The prodigal in this poem is still at the point in his life where he is in trouble.

■ Activity 5: 'Mother to Son' by Langston Hughes

This poem has the following elements:

- An (imaginary) crystal stair.
- An actual staircase which is bare wood and marred by tacks and splinters.
- The mother has been climbing the staircase.
- There are corners to be turned.
- Often there is darkness.

Together these elements work to create the staircase as a symbol of the pathway to success in life. A crystal staircase would be one which conferred wealth, perhaps, and success on the person lucky enough to climb it. The staircase that this woman must climb, however, is full of obstacles. The tacks and splinters can hurt her. There are corners, which suggest that she cannot always see what lies ahead. Sometimes she finds herself in darkness, which, again, suggests she cannot see what to do or where to go. The staircase is a symbol of a hard life, but one in which the mother has the will and the courage to keep climbing. The narrator offers it to her son as incentive for him to do the same – keep climbing. Upward is the direction of success.

■ Activity 6: 'Adam Cast Forth' by Jorge Luis Borges

The reference here to the Garden of Eden is first of all the literal garden from the Bible story. The speaker is Adam (which we know from the title), and he is speaking long after he was expelled from the garden (which we know because the memory of the garden has faded). The garden here, as expected, is set up as paradise, and it is contrasted with the world in which Adam now lives. That world is characterized as being stubborn and incestuous – so fraught with immorality. The speaker tells us that he expects never to return to the garden – never to return to paradise – but he finishes the poem by saying that the memory of the love and the joy he experienced in the garden sustains him. The poem gives us the idea that mankind cannot live in paradise, but can feed its spirit with memories of the love and joy that we do experience, though we experience them for short periods of time.

■ Activity 7: 'Legend' by Judith Wright

Possible symbols in the poem include the following:

- **Rifle**: possibly a symbol of death, but may also be a symbol of something that the boy can use to defend himself.

- **Black dog**: another symbol of death. The dog is black, and Cerebus, the guardian of the gateway to Hell, is a dog. This dog is chasing at the boy's heels, which suggests that danger is following him.

- **Cobwebs**: we associate cobwebs with abandoned spaces that spiders have taken over. The image of cobwebs draped over walls and doorways calls up the idea of desolation.

- **Rivers**: rivers are water, which can be symbols of rebirth; however, in the context of this poem, the rivers are presented as obstacles, keeping the boy from getting where he wants to be.

- **Thorn branches**: thorns are connected to the crucifixion of Jesus Christ; he was given a thorn wreath to wear on his head. Thorns are sharp and cause injury. In the context of this poem, the thorns are causing blindness.

- **Blindness**: a symbol of the inability to see one's way.

- **Unlucky opal**: the opal has a complicated history. It was considered lucky for centuries, but then came to be considered unlucky. The fire in the stone has been seen as ominous.

All of these symbols together suggest that the blacksmith's boy is on a dangerous journey which might lead to his death. The last lines of the stanza, however, show him defying the dangers and he declares himself ready to meet all challenges. The number of dangers that lie on his journey serves to heighten the strength of his confidence in himself when he claims he can overcome all of them.

■ Activity 8: Structure in Lorna Goodison's 'Farewell Wild Woman (I)'

In the first two lines, the narrator asserts that she has put the wild woman – evidently a part of her own personality – aside. In lines 3–7, she details the reasons that the wild woman had to be put away. Lines 9–16 are all one sentence, and in it we see that the speaker's determination to put the wild woman aside is at some risk. She describes the wild woman sneaking about outside in the bushes – not far away. In terms of structure, then, we can see that the speaker's confidence shakes as she goes along. She begins with a firm statement, but in remembering the aspects of the wild woman, she begins to slip from her determination to put the wild woman away. The fact that more than half the poem consists of a description of the wild woman hovering just outside of the speaker's safe zone (represented by her house) suggests that the determination to keep the wild woman away is doomed to failure. We end up getting the impression that the speaker is trapped in the house with the wild woman lurking outside.

■ Activity 9: 'Unready to Wear' by Kurt Vonnegut, Jr

■ Narrator

We have a first-person narrator here who is talking about his own life. He seems to be claiming that he lives in a world in which 'people' have no bodies but can borrow physical bodies if they want to go about in the world and do physical things. Such a claim seems to be quite mad, of course; however, since we are familiar with science fiction as a genre, we can immediately recognize that the author is working in that genre and is not trying to write about the physical world as we know it. We have, therefore, no reason from this excerpt to think that the narrator is unreliable. His presentation seems quite balanced; he recognizes his wife's excitement over being able to wear a beautiful body, and he recognizes that her experience is different from his own. He is able to describe Konigswasser as a genius and a very kind man; he does not revile him because his body was somewhat defective.

■ Symbols and metaphors

The idea of being 'amphibious' might be symbolic of being reborn, although the water is evidently not literal. In fact, since we discover that these people have been reborn into creatures without bodies, the reference to water is quite logical. Blonde hair seems to be a symbol, at least to Madge, of physical beauty. That is an idea with which we are still quite familiar in Western society. Within the culture of the story, the parade is a symbol of Konigswasser's achievement, which tells us that the inhabitants of this culture revere him and so are obviously quite happy with their non-corporeal situation. Konigswasser's choice to march as a six-foot cowboy who can bend beer cans tells us that he is drawn to the symbol of a very masculine sort of man, a stereotype of strong, adventurous men. We don't know where this story is going, but we see that in a quite imaginative society in which people have no physical bodies, they are drawn to traditional ideas of physical beauty.

■ Structure

The narrator moves around in time, for example:

- He begins in the present, describing a routine of his society – the obligation to go work in the storage centers. He then goes on to describe some ongoing features of life in his society in describing the way that the women, including his wife, behave.

- Then he flashes back to when he and his wife had bodies by way of contrasting her real body with her choice of bodies in her new life. By line 19, then, the narrator has moved from generalities about his society to the specific effect the change to the 'amphibious' state has had on his wife.

- He then moves to a contrast: the way he, and most men, have reacted to the situation of being able to choose a body. He follows a similar pattern to what he did with his description of his wife: he talks about what he chooses, and what his wife chooses for him, then flashes back to a description of what his own physical body was like.

- In the next section of the passage, the narrator returns to a description of a cultural practice: the annual parade in honour of Konigswasser. Just about half the passage is dedicated to this description, so it takes on the focus as the most important idea, the thing to which the narrator has been building.

- The passage ends with a characterization of Konigswasser in terms of his own reaction to having a choice of bodies. Konigswasser's attitude seems to be different from most men.

Overall in the passage, then, the structure seems to help the narrator accomplish several things: we get a contrast between people's experience now, in the body-less society, and their experience in the past, when they all had bodies. He also contrasts the women's attitudes with the men's attitudes, and he establishes an image of the cultural values as expressed through a major cultural ritual. We don't know where the story is going, but the narrator has used the structure to set up some important contrasts and to give a basis for understanding the values of the world in the story.

Chapter 4: Approaches to visual texts

◼ Activity 1: Verbal-visual interplay in advertisements

There is a lot going on in both of the texts presented in this activity, so we will only focus on a few major points here. We will consider the texts in comparison to one another.

The first text makes use of perspective to draw our attention to the electrical plug at the center of the advertisement; then our eye travels down to the car attached to the end of the cable. This secondary emphasis on the car suggests that the target audience is people who are environmentally conscious and not necessarily car enthusiasts. This is unlike the 1947 advertisement, which places emphasis on the car itself, suggestive of a more materialistic audience.

You might also have picked up on the different assumptions that are made about the target audience in each of the ads. The 1947 ad directly 'speaks' to its audience by using the personal pronoun 'you'. It is clear through the images placed throughout the text that this 'you' is a man. We see men engaging in stereotypically masculine activities (fishing, hunting, visiting the barber, reading the newspaper); even when we look into the car, we see a woman (presumably the wife) in the passenger seat, with a young child in the backseat, emphasising the car's appeal to the 'family man'. The modern ad, however, is gender neutral in both verbal and visual language. Not only is there no use of personal pronouns, but there are also no images of a potential buyer. In this way, the ad avoids making any assumptions about gender, class or age and thus appeals to a wider market.

The style of the two ads is also interesting when compared with one another. The original ad looks like a hand-drawn sketch, whereas the more modern ad is clearly digitally altered. These differences reflect not just the evolution of technology but also of Chevrolet as a brand. Whereas at one time the company may have focused on the size of the car (the text also emphasises this 'bigger, better' message), 60 years later Chevrolet's focus has shifted to acknowledging their responsibility to the environment, showing their understanding of the changing demands of their target market. The style is kind of ironic; the more basic drawing emphasises a natural backdrop while delivering a consumerist message, whereas the more 'flashy' digital artwork reflects a more environmentally friendly message.

◼ Activity 2: Juxtaposition in *Persepolis*

On the surface, the images in each panel seem to mirror each other. However, the first panel depicts the grim fate of young martyrs who have been promised a better life in exchange for their sacrifice for the cause of the revolution. The narrator, Marji, is roughly the same age as the boys in the first image and is depicted in the far right corner of the page. She is in a much more privileged position and is naive (but not oblivious) to the exploitation of these young boys, as evidenced by the expression of wide-eyed excitement on her face. Marji and her partying friends willingly rip holes in their clothes and accessorize with items that are usually associated with weaponry and torture (chains and nails) in an effort to look cool. Their appearances provide a stark contrast to the illustration above which shows the martyrs literally being ripped apart – a consequence of accepting the key, which in the end symbolizes death, not the better life that they were promised. The movements of the bodies in each panel are also duplicated, but this is ironic; in one case, those movements are tragic, and in the other the movements reflect the happy mood of the partygoers.

■ Activity 3: Graphic elements in *The Arrival*

In comparison to *Maus* and *Persepolis*, which have more of a comic-book style, the images here are much more life-like. The colour scheme adds to this effect. Tan has stated that:

> the style of the artwork borrows heavily from old sepia/monochrome photographs of the kind that typically document social life during the nineteenth and early twentieth centuries, and to some extent the book behaves like a silent film.

You might also have noticed the use of emanata. The subjects in the images show a mixture of emotions: sadness, worry, expectation. These emotions are depicted in a more realistic manner than in more comic-style graphic novels, but we can certainly 'read' the emotions in the facial expressions.

Finally, you might have picked up on the use of the origami bird as a visual symbol. Unless you are familiar with the whole text, this one extract does not provide enough context for you to understand the symbol's greater significance, but its emphasis in several of the panels (especially its salience in the last panel on the left hand page) should give you a clue (perhaps a form of visual foreshadowing) that it will be important. You could consider some generic symbolic associations with birds (eg, they represent freedom, mobility, perspective) and connect this to what you know about the text, but you would need to read further to see if these ideas are supported by the rest of the narrative.

■ Activity 4: Symbols in political cartoons

In the first cartoon, Breen uses the image of a bubble to represent the tenuous future of Bitcoin, the controversial cryptocurrency which reached a peak value of almost $20 000 per one Bitcoin in 2018. We can infer that the bubble will soon burst. As the value of the Bitcoin keeps going up and up (metaphorically, but also depicted literally in the image), so too does the probability that it will not last.

In the second cartoon, an allusion is made to the famous nursery rhyme of Humpty Dumpty. The wall that is referred to here is the border wall between the United States and Mexico, an issue that was at the centre of President Donald Trump's campaign and became a focus of his presidency in late 2018. In December 2018, conflicts over funding for the wall resulted in a partial shutdown of the federal government, which is what the cartoon is depicting. The cartoon is suggesting that it is Trump's persistence over the issue that will cause his own downfall.

■ **Works cited**
Tan, Shaun, *The Arrival*, Hodder Children's Books, London, 2007 (print).

Chapter 5: Writing about texts

■ Activity 1: Writing a summary and an analysis

Here is one possible summary of the article 'Colin Kaepernick's national anthem protest' by Ijeoma Oluo:

Ijeoma Oluo tells the story of Colin Kaepernick and his protest against the oppression of black people. She explains how Kaepernick did not want to stand by silently, so he decided to sit during the national anthem. She then explains that the protest created a lot of controversy, and she summarizes several of the arguments that detractors brought forth against him. She then makes the claim that all of the arguments are wrong, and she goes on to detail, for each one, why it is wrong. She ends by praising Kaepernick for his bravery and claiming that what he did actually stands for American values, rather than undermining it.

In terms of analysis, here are some of the techniques you might have decided to discuss:

- **Structure**: the writer sets up the problem of the controversy surrounding Kaepernick's protest, she identifies the arguments that people who oppose him have been using and then she systematically shoots each one down. She ends by drawing a bigger conclusion than 'Kaepernick is right'; she identifies his actions as emblematic of deeply held American values.

- **Anecdote**: Oluo uses the anecdote of Kaepernick's protest as a means of highlighting the social problem of racism.

- **Social commentary**: the article is focused on the presence and effects of racism in the United States today, and so a discussion of social context would be insightful in terms of understanding the nature of the text.

- **Use of facts**: these are used to counter emotional claims.

- **Narrative perspective**: the author is herself black and so has a personal stake in what Kaepernick's protest is about. That personal perspective lends weight to her argument, since she knows from personal experience the reality of what is being protested.

Other techniques could have been analysed, so if you identified some that are not on this list, but you can support your claims with text from the article and you can connect the techniques to the meaning of the text, then your choices are as valid as those presented here.

■ Activity 2: 'May' by John Shaw Neilson

In terms of summary, you should note that there is very little in the way of action here. This is a lyric poem, and the point is to create an effect – a feeling about the coming of the month of May. The summary, therefore, would consist of a statement about what Neilson describes.

The analysis in this case would probably focus on imagery, which is possibly the most significant poetic technique that Neilson used here. You could also discuss structure, the use of rhyme and the use of the first-person perspective. You may wish to consider the use of contrast between the brown earth uncovered by the plough and the bright colours of spring mentioned in the rest of the poem.

■ Activity 3: Analysing structure in an infographic

Some of the significant elements in the infographic of the Thai football team include:

- The use of the figures of the divers and the child to convey a clear understanding of the mechanism used by rescuers.

- The labelling of the parts to help the viewer, who might not be a diver, to understand the elements of the rescue.

- The title.

- The use of colour to differentiate between the divers and the soccer players. Of particular interest is the fact that we can see that the child's oxygen tank was carried by the lead diver so as to avoid any problems for the inexperienced diver.

- The use of the brown colour at the top and bottom of the infographic to create the effect of the cave.

A generalization about structure might read something like this:

The infographic relies primarily on the structural device of colour and physical orientation of elements of the diagram to help convey to the viewer how the rescue of the Thai soccer players was successfully effected.

■ Activity 4: Analysing narrative perspective

Question	Answer
Who is the speaker?	The speaker is King George VI, the King of England at the outbreak of the Second World War.
When is the speaker talking?	The King is speaking at the moment of England's becoming directly involved in the war.
How is the speaker speaking?	The King is speaking solemnly. He makes calm assertions, acknowledging the difficulty of the times to come and the seriousness of the events about which he is speaking, but he also asks the nation to see the war as something 'right', and he offers encouragement that England will be able to prevail.
What is the speaker's relationship to the events about which he or she is speaking?	The King is the leader of the country, and so he carries the direct responsibility of setting the tone for the nation. People will model their attitudes toward and actions regarding the war on his. This is a great responsibility, of which he is evidently aware.
Description of narrative perspective	The narrative perspective is first-person and the speaker is a person with a very high level of involvement in his subject. He is, however, a leader with tremendous responsibility, so care has been taken that what he says he believes. The bias is not personal, but rather the bias of what is good for the nation.

■ Activity 5: Evaluating thesis statements

	Statement	Numbers of the tips that this statement violates
A	In 'Once More to the Lake', EB White shows that he loved the lake as a child.	1 and 2
B	In 'Once More to the Lake', EB White tells us about the lake he used to go to as a child, gives us details of what the lake was like then, and then gives us details of what the lake is like now.	1, 2 and 5
C	In 'Once More to the Lake', EB White shows that the recognition of one's own mortality is a devastating experience that changes our vision of ourselves in a fundamental way.	This is an effective thesis statement.
D	In 'Once More to the Lake', EB White uses symbolism, flashback, and anecdote to make his point.	1, 4 and 6
E	In 'Once More to the Lake,' EB White writes about death.	1 and 6
F	EB White's 'Once More to the Lake' shows that memory, nostalgia, confusion and death.	3

This is the claim. The rest of the paragraph must substantiate it. ⎯

This is the evidence. Notice that the facts are given in enough detail to ensure that the reader can understand what happened and that what happened was accidental, rather than the result of deliberate research.

■ Activity 6: Identifying C-E-W in a sample paragraph

Sometimes valuable discoveries are not made from deliberate investigation, but rather by chance. Andrew Nalbandov, who discovered that hypophysectomized chickens—chickens whose pituitary glands have been removed (Dixon 31)—died unless they were exposed to a minimum of two one-hour periods of light nightly (Dixon 32). This discovery occurred as the result of a serendipitous event: a substitute janitor working at the research facility preferred to leave the lights on all night. By a second lucky chance, Nalbandov discovered the difference between this janitor's habits and those of the regular janitor, and noted that while the substitute janitor was on duty, Nalbandov's chickens did not die (Dixon 32). The knowledge Nalbandov gained was invaluable to him—a string of dead chickens resulted only in negative knowledge and stalled the experiment—but it was not gained as the result of a difficult process. Luck is sometimes a primary mechanism in the making of scientific knowledge, and often, as in this case and in the more famous case of the discovery of penicillin, the knowledge gained is highly valued, but not because of any particular difficulty in attaining it.

The pink indicates the warrant. The warrant explains how the accidental discovery that Nalbandov made demonstrates the point that some important (valuable) discoveries are made by chance. The initial claim on which the paragraph was made was that some discoveries occur by chance, so this example is an effective one.

■ Activity 7: Evaluating analytical writing and identifying C-E-W

Some observations you might make about this essay are as follows:

- The essay does answer the question as it was asked, but it does so in an interesting way. Part of the question is answered in the introduction and thesis (the part about Bryson's purpose). The part of the question which asks about audience is not answered until the concluding paragraph. Dividing the answer that way can be an effective strategy so long as the argument builds to the conclusion and the conclusion is not simply tacked on at the end without relating to the rest of the essay.

- The introduction is very short – this is satisfactory when writing in timed circumstances.

- The body paragraphs do effectively use the claim-evidence-warrant structure to make their points.

- The question suggests that the writer should discuss stylistic technique where appropriate, and this essay builds in discussion of blunt diction, use of anecdote and use of sarcasm.

- The writer of the essay shows that he or she has a sophisticated understanding of the text because he or she has been able to see a much larger context for the writing than the narrow effort to discredit one sports personality: the essay is seen as a commentary on the importance of accuracy in the making of historical knowledge. That greater context explains Bryson's motivation for making a concerted effort to wreck the reputation of someone who was once very popular.

Glossary

Allusion: a reference to something without a literal or explicit mention of it.

Analogy: a comparison between two unlike things presented as a way of furthering a line of reasoning or to support an argument.

Analysis: the reader's observation of how the narrator is telling the story, the identification of the various elements of that story-telling process, and the explanation of how those elements create meaning.

Anecdote: an interesting or humorous story about a real-life event.

Antagonist: a character who is working consciously to stop the protagonist from implementing his or her plan.

Appeal: a persuasive technique split into three types: ethos, logos and pathos.

Audience: the intended readership of a text.

Ballad: a poem of short stanzas that narrates a story, often arranged in quatrains.

Bias: unbalanced language that suggests support for a particular ideological view and/or group of people.

Block-by-block: an essay technique whereby you write all your analysis of one work and then all your analysis of the other work.

C-E-W (claim, evidence, warrant): the claim is the statement of what you intend to demonstrate in the paragraph which ties back to the topic of the essay. The evidence is the information from the text that supports the claim. The warrant is the explanation of your thinking.

Climax: in drama, the final complication that determines whether the plan is going to be successful or not.

Complication: in drama, something that arises as a result of the protagonist's effort to implement the plan, and which interferes with the ability to employ the plan effectively.

Composition: in a visual text, everything that is included or omitted from an image.

Conflict: a struggle between two opposing forces.

Content: the literal meaning of the text; what happens.

Couplet: two lines in a poem that typically rhyme and are of the same length and metre.

Diction: the words chosen in a text.

Disturbance: in drama, something that occurs to upset the balance and force the character(s) to deal with an unexpected problem.

Dramatic irony: when the audience knows something that the characters in the play do not.

Dramatic situation: the situation in which the actions of the story occur.

Ethos: an ethical appeal to the authority of the writer or speaker.

Extended metaphor: a metaphor used throughout a poem or a lengthy passage, often to point out certain characteristics of the subject for the reader to consider.

Fabula: a fictional world created by the writer.

Figurative language: language that uses figures of speech, such as metaphors or symbols, to embellish meaning beyond the literal.

First-person narration: the author/narrator as an active participant in the experience he or she is sharing, not a passive observer.

Free verse: an open form of poetry that has no formal or recognized structure.

Hyperbole: exaggeration to make a situation seem more dramatic or humorous.

Implied author: the author that the text implies, constructed through reading.

Irony: using words or phrases to convey an intended meaning different from the literal meaning, or in contrast to the expected meaning.

Jargon: words that are used in a specific context that may be difficult to understand and often involving technical terminology.

Juxtaposition: the contrast of two unrelated objects, images or ideas placed next to each other.

Lexical sets: a group of words that are related to each other in meaning, for example, leaf, green, trunk, bark and branch would all be part of the same lexical set in relation to the word 'tree'.

Literary device: a technique or tool that a writer uses to create an effect; examples include imagery and personification.

Logos: an appeal to logic.

Manifesto: a written statement of the beliefs, aims and policies of an organization, especially a political party.

Metaphor: a comparison between two things.

Metre: the arrangement of stressed and unstressed syllables in a line of a poem or a verse.

Monologue: an (often long) speech given by one person or character.

Mood: the feeling that is evoked in the reader (or audience) as a result of the tone that is set.

Narrative perspective: the way a story is being told and from whose point of view.

Narrative situation: the situation in which the narrator tells the story.

Negative space: in art, the space around a subject. Providing a lot of negative space often gives more focus to a subject.

Obstacle: something that already exists in the fictional situation, which interferes with the protagonist's ability to implement his or her plan.

Octet: an eight-line stanza.

Ode: a lyrical poem usually without a regular metre.

Opening balance: the situation in the fictional world at the beginning of a play.

Pastiche: an imitation of another piece of work.

Pathos: an appeal to emotion.

Perspective: in art and photography, this refers to the depth and spatial relationships between objects.

Petrarchan sonnet: a sonnet consisting of an octet followed by a sestet – eight lines followed by six lines. The rhyme scheme is 'abba', 'abba', 'cde', 'cde'. You will see several variations of the 'cde' rhymes, however.

Plot: a series of events that are linked causally.

Point-by-point: a technique in essay writing that takes each point and analyses how each one is used in both texts before you move on to the next point.

Propaganda: information presented in a biased way to influence the reader, often to promote a political cause or ideology.

Protagonist: in drama, the character who has the plan for dealing with the disturbance.

Purpose: what the text sets out to achieve; why the text is created.

Quatrain: a stanza of four lines.

Register: the level of formality in writing or speaking.

Reliable narrator: a trustworthy narrator who presents what the author thinks, believes, feels or values accurately.

Repetition: the repeated use of a word, phrase or image to draw attention to it.

Resolution: in drama, the outcome that brings a new balance.

Rhetoric: language designed to convince or persuade, making good use of compositional techniques.

Rhetorical devices: compositional techniques and tools that a speaker uses, eg, analogy.

Rhetorical question: a question that implies an answer, which is a subtle way of persuading someone or influencing someone's opinion.

Rhyme: the repetition of two or more similar sounds, often occurring at the ends of a line in poetry.

Rule of thirds: a compositional technique used in photography whereby the photograph (or image) is divided into thirds, with the dominant part of the image (the subject, or focus) positioned at one of the points of intersection.

Salience: when referring to an image, means the dominant part of the image, or that which first attracts the eye's attention.

Semantic fields: a collection of words or phrases that are related to each other in meaning and connotation, for example, safety, welcome, support, shelter, structure and warmth would all be part of the same semantic field in relation to the word home.

Sestet: a six-line stanza.

Sestina: a complex verse form with six stanzas of six lines and a final triplet. All stanzas have the same six words at the line ends in six different sequences. The final triplet contains all six words.

Structure: the way in which a text is organized (it is not the same thing as layout).

Style: how the text conveys its meaning; the way in which the content is presented.

Stylistic devices: tools that an author uses to achieve an intended effect, for example, metaphor or rhetoric.

Summary: the description of the events of the dramatic situation.

Suspense: a feeling from the audience when waiting for an outcome.

Symbol: a comparison between something the author wants the reader to think about and another element, often discussed as a subset of the category of metaphor.

Syntax: the arrangement of words in a sentence or text.

Tenor: in relation to a metaphor, the tenor is the thing or object that the author wants the reader to understand better.

Tone: the attitude of the writer or speaker towards his or her subject.

Unreliable narrator: an untrustworthy narrator who does not speak in accordance with the author's intentions.

Vehicle: in relation to a metaphor, the vehicle is the thing or object that the author is comparing their subject to.

Villanelle: a poem of 19 lines, with only two rhymes throughout, and some lines repeated.

Volta: a significant turn in the direction of a poem.

Index

Acknowledgements

The Publishers would like to thank the following for permission to reproduce copyright material.

Every effort has been made to trace all copyright holders, but if any have been inadvertently overlooked, the Publishers will be pleased to make the necessary arrangements at the first opportunity.

Photo credits:

t = top   *m* = middle   *b* = bottom   *r* = right   *l* = left

p.22 *tl and bl* © Oxford Dictionaries, Oxford University Press 2019; *mr* © tostphoto/stock.adobe.com; **p.23** *tl* © John Frost Newspapers/Alamy Stock Photo, *tm* © John Frost Newspapers/Alamy Stock Photo, *tr* © John Frost Newspapers/Alamy Stock Photo, *mr* © John Parrot/Stocktrek Images, Inc./Alamy Stock Photo; **p.28** © Oxfam International; **p.34** © Alan Holden; **p.56** *top from left to right* © Sylvie Bouchard/stock.adobe.com, © Md3d/stock.adobe.com, © Figura13/stock.adobe.com, © Michele Paccione/Shutterstock.com; **p.69** © Michael L. Baird, flickr.bairdphotos.com, https://creativecommons.org/licenses/by/2.0/; **p.70** *t* © Serghei Velusceac/stock.adobe.com, *bl* © Dior, *br* © https://commons.wikimedia.org/wiki/File:Allisvanity.jpg, https://creativecommons.org/publicdomain/zero/1.0/; **p.71** *t* Courtesy Pest Control Office, Banksy, Show Me The Monet, 2005; *b* © The Frontier Post; **p.72** © Steve Bell; **p.73** both © Chevrolet; **p.77** *t* © Gift of Philip van Ingen, 1942/Metropolitan Museum of Art, *b* © Steve Bell; **p.78** *t* © Steve Breen, *m* © Mike Luckovich

Text credits:

pp.8–10 'To Speak Another Language Isn't Just Cultured, It's A Blow Against Stupidity' by Michael Hofmann, The Guardian, 15 Aug 2010. Reprinted with permission; **p.15** © Elizabeth Gilbert, 2009, *Eat Pray Love: One Woman's Search for Everything*, Bloomsbury Publishing Plc.; 'Book Three: Indonesia' from *Eat Pray Love: One Woman's Search for Everything Across Italy, India and Indonesia* by Elizabeth Gilbert, copyright © 2006 by Elizabeth Gilbert. Used by permission of Viking Books, an imprint of Penguin Publishing Group, a division of Penguin Random House LLC. All rights reserved; **p.19** 'Letter To Susan Owen', by Owen, Wilfred (1893-1918). The Harry Ransom Center / The Wilfred Owen Literary Estate via First World War Poetry Digital Archive, accessed February 7, 2019, http://ww1lit.nsms.ox.ac.uk/ww1lit/collections/document/5262; **p.21** With permission from Dr EDF Williams; **p.22** Meera Dolasia. "Oxford Dictionaries 'Word Of The Year' Is . . . An Emoji?" DOGOnews, DOGO Media, Inc., 17 Nov, 2015, www.dogonews.com/2015/11/17/oxford-dictionaries-word-of-the-year-is-an-emoji. Accessed 19 Jun. 2019. Reproduced with the permission of DOGO Media, Inc; **pp.25–26** Excerpted from 'The Art of Biography" from *The Death of the Moth and Other Essays* by Virginia Wcolf. Copyright © 1942 by Houghtori Mifflin Harcourt Publishing Conspany, renewed 1970 by MarjorieT. Parsons. Executrix. Reprinted by permission of Houghton Mifflin Harcourt Publishing Company. All rights reserved. 'The Art of Biography' from *The Death of the Moth, and Other Essays* by Virginia Woolf, Chapter 23. From ebooks website, accessed 3 December 2018. Reproduced with the permission of The Society of Authors as the literary Representative of the Estate of Virginia Woolf; **p.26** 'It's Alive' – blog post from Meg Gardiner's blog 'Lying for a Living'. Posted on 27 July 2006 © Meg Gardiner; **p.29** extract from 'Propaganda is Everywhere – Propaganda Critic' by Aaron Delwich (2018). Accessed 3 December 2018. Reproduced with the permission from Aaron Delwich; **pp.29–30** Women's Equality Party; **p.31** Quote from a speech by Margaret Thatcher 'The Lady's Not For Turning.' Reproduced with permission from Margaret Thatcher Archives Trust. Extract from Henry Kissinger's memo to President Richard Nixon, 10 September 1969, expressing his reservations about prospects for 'Vietnamization' of the conflict in Vietnam. Office of the Historian, Bureau of Public Affairs. Quote from Hillary Clinton's 1996 Democratic National Convention Address. Reproduced with permission; **p.33** Extract from Tom Brokaw's World War II Memorial Dedication Address. Reproduced with the permission of NBCUniversal. Extract from Barak Obama's Election Night Victory Speech (4 November 2008). Accessed 28 Jan 2019. Reproduced with the perission from The Office of Barack and Michelle Obama; **pp.34–35** An interview with Minoli Salgado by Ira Ansari for The Missing Slate: Art & Literary Journal (published Jan 2014). https://themissingslate.com/2014/01/18/author-of-the-month-minoli-salgado/. Reproduced with the permission of the Magazine "The Missing Slate."; **pp.36–37** 'The Case for Ending Social Media' by Henry N Brooks – article on The Harvard Crimson website. Accessed 19 Nov 2018. www.thecrimson.com/column/socially-liberal-fiscally-liberal/article/2018/2/6/brooks-ending-social-media/. Reproduced with the permission of The Harvard Crimson, Inc.; **p.41** 'Lost in Translation' from *Wild Ducks Flying Backward* by Tom Robbins, copyright© 2005 by Tom Robbins. Used by permission of Bantam Books, an imprint of Random House, a division of Penguin Random House LLC. All rights reserved. Quote from 'Lost in Translation' (pp209–11) in *Wild Ducks Flying Backward: the Short Writings of Tom Robbins*, by Tom Robbins, published by Bantam Books (2006). Reproduced with the permission from No Exit Press cleared through PLS clear.; **pp.42–43** 'My Last Duchess' by Robert Browning; **p.43** extract from *The Tell-Tale Heart* by Edgar Allen Poe. The Poe Museum; **pp.44–45** extract from Cyrano de Bergerac by Edmond Rostand. The Project Gutenberg Ebook of Cyrano de Bergerac; **p.46** extract from 'Showing or Telling: Narrators in the Drama of Tennessee Williams. *American Literature*, Vol. 51, No. 1, March 1979, pp.84–93, doi:10.2307/2924921; **p.50** excerpts from 'The Prodigal' from *Poems* by Elizabeth Bishop. Copyright © 2011 by The Alice H. Methfessel Trust. Publisher's Note and compilation copyright © 2011 by Farrar, Straus and Giroux; (Chatto&Windus credit line); **p.51** Excerpts from 'The Fish' from *Poems* by Elizabeth Bishop. Copyright © 2011 by The Alice H. Methfessel Trust. Publisher's Note and compilation copyright © 2011 by Farrar, Straus and Giroux. Excerpts from 'The Fish' and 'The Prodiga' from POEMS by Elizabeth Bishop. Copyright © 2011 by The Alice H. Methfessel Trust. Publisher's Note and compilation copyright © 2011 by Farrar, Straus and Giroux. Reprinted by permission of Chatto & Windus in UK and commonwealth.; **p.52** 'Mother to Son' by Langston Hughes from *The Collected Poems of Langston Hughes*. Edited by Arnold Rampersad, Vintage Books (1995). Copyright © 1994 by The Estate of Langston Hughes. Reprinted with the permission of David Higham Associates.; 'Mother to Son' from *The Collected Poems of Langston Hughes* by Langston Hughes, edited by Arnold Rampersad with David Roessel, Associate Editor, copyright © 1994 by the Estate of Langston Hughes. Used by permission of Alfred A. Knopf, an imprint of the Knopf Doubleday Publishing Group, a division of Penguin Random House LLC. All rights reserved; **p.53** From *Wit's End: What Wit Is, How It Works, And Why We Need It* by James Geary. Copyright © 2019 by James Geary. Used by permission of W. W. Norton & Company, Inc.; **pp.53–54** Excerpt from 'Everything That Rises Must Converge' from *The Complete Stories* by Flannery O'Connor. Copyright © 1971 by the Estate of Mary Flannery O'Connor; Extract from 'Everything that Rises Must Converge' by Flannery O'Connor reprinted by permission of Peters Fraser & Dunlop (www.petersfraserdunlop.com) on behalf of the Estate of Flannery O'Connor; **p.55** 'Adam Cast Out' by Jorge Luis Borges. All Poetry (www.Allpoetry.com) Copyright information provided: Translated by Genia Gurarie, 4.1. Copyright retained by Genia Gurarie; **p.56** Judith Wright, Collected Poems and HarperCollins Publishers for giving permission to reprint the text; **pp.57–58** Extract from 'The Garden Party' in *Katherine Mansfield Short Stories*, by Katherine Mansfield.; **p.61** 'Demetor' from *New Selected Poems 1984-2004* by Carol Ann Dully. Published by Picador, 2004 Copyright © Carol Ann Duffy. Reproduced by permission of the author do Rogers, Coleridge & White Ltd., 20 Powis Mews, London Wil IJN; **pp.62–63** From Birth of the Owl Butterflies by Ruth Sharman, Picador, 1997. Reproduced with the permission from Ruth Sharman; **pp.64–65** Selected poems by Goodison, Lorna, Reproduced with permission of University of Michigan Press in the format Book via Copyright Clearance Center; **pp.65–66** UNREADY TO WEAR by Kurt Vonnegut. Copyright © Kurt Vonnegut Jr. 1950, 1951, 1953, 1954, 1955, 1956, 1958, 1960, 1961, 1962, 1964, 1966, 1968, used by permission of The Wylie Agency (UK) Limited. UNREADY TO WEAR by Kurt Vonnegut. Copyright © Kurt Vonnegut Jr. 1950, 1951, 1953, 1954, 1955, 1956, 1958, 1960, 1961, 1962, 1964, 1966, 1968, used by permission Penguin Random House LLC. All Right Reserved; **p.76** British Museum text accompanying an 1805 cartoon 'The plumb-pudding in danger – or – State Epicures taking un Petit Souper' by James Gillray. Accessed 13 December 2018; **p.81** Letter written by Sullivan Ballou, Judge Advocate of the Rhode Island militia during the American Civil War. Edited by Ken Burns, PBS: The Civil War, (2015); **pp.85–86** Colin Kaepernick's national anthem protest is fundamentally American by Ijeoma Oluo, *The Guardian*, 29 August 2016. Reprinted with permission of Guardian News and Media Ltd.; **pp.87–88** 'The Girl with the Black

Hair' by Australian poet John Shaw Neilson from Collected Poems published by Lothian Book Publishing Company in 1934; **p.89** 'May' by John Shaw Neilson from Collected Poems published by Lothian Book Publishing Company in 1934; **p.92** Letter written by Sullivan Ballou, Judge Advocate of the Rhode Island militia during the American Civil War. Edited by Ken Burns, PBS: The Civil War, (2015); **pp.94–96** From 'Hole in the Sky' from *Two Poems by Niyi Osundare*, published in World Literature Today, 15 September 2014. Reproduced with the permission from Niyi Osundare; **p.99** An extract from the article headed 'Should Any Vaccines Be Required for Children?' from ProCon.org – Understand the Issues Understand Each Other, 23 July 2018. Used with permission from ProCon.org.; **p.100** Extract from the opening passage of *The Songlines* by Bruce Chatwin published by Picador (1987). Used by permission from Penguin Random House UK, a division of Penguin Random House LLC. All rights reserved.; **pp.101-2** Speech given by King George VI on 3 September 1939. 'The King Speaks: There May Be Dark Days Ahead'. Ibiblio. org. The U.S. National Archives and Records Administration.; **p.114** Extract from an article entitled 'Bill Stern: The Greatest Mythmaker of Them All' by Bill Bryson Sr (father of Bill Bryson). Reproduced with the permission of Bill Bryson.